Shared Fate has become a classic. When it appeared in 1964 it sent a shock wave through the adoption mystique, much as Betty Friedan's book had done for the feminine mystique. David Kirk's researches had demonstrated that not everything was well with the way adoptive parents tended to deal with their child-rearing tasks. Their problems seemed in part derived from misconceptions then propagated by popular writers and even by professional personnel.

Shared Fate went beyond telling the truth about the adoptive family as different from a mythical 'normal' family of two parents with children created by them. It went further by showing that 'difference' could serve the adoptive family as an asset. Thus, when parents close ranks with their children's atypical status in society by acknowledging their own atypical status, they help to create a family of strong parent-child bonds. This discovery derived from ten years of meticulous researches involving some 2,000 adoptive families in Canada and the United States.

Shared Fate has stood the test of time. Even though new forms of adoption have emerged and become numerically dominant, the book's findings remain pertinent for all the parties involved: adoptive parents, adoptees, birthparents, social agencies and the courts.

Shared Fate

A THEORY AND METHOD OF ADOPTIVE RELATIONSHIPS

H. David Kirk

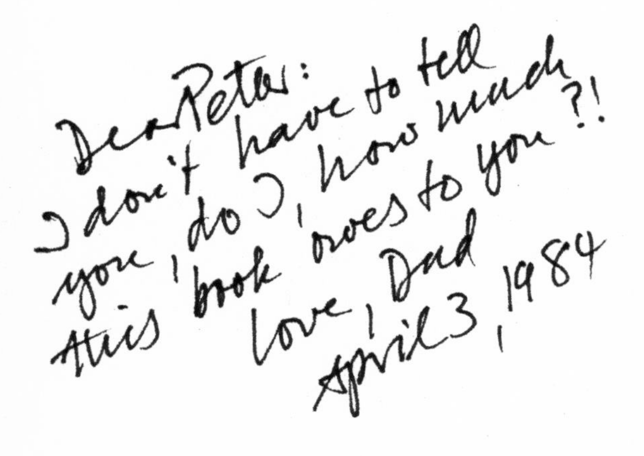

Ben-Simon Publications
Port Angeles, Washington
Brentwood Bay, British Columbia

Revised Edition 1984

Ben-Simon Publications

USA: P.O. Box 2124
Port Angeles, WA 98362
Canada: P.O. Box 318
Brentwood Bay, B.C. V0S 1A0

Library of Congress Catalog Card Number: 63-16589
ISBN 0-914539-00-0
(Original ISBN 0-02-917340-X by Free Press, NY, 1964)

PRINTED AND BOUND IN USA

TO DEBBIE, BILL, FRANCIE AND PETER
AND TO ALL THEIR PARENTS

. . . a society which must carry out more complicated processes based upon thinking and acting with a purpose in view, will, in certain situations, necessarily tend to produce the reflective type of person. From this point of view it is clearly fallacious to regard reflectiveness—as many romantic thinkers do—as being under all circumstances a life-extinguishing force. On the contrary, in most cases, reflectiveness preserves life by helping us to adjust ourselves to new situations so complex that in them the naive and unreflective man would be utterly at a loss.

—KARL MANNHEIM (1950, 57)

Contents

APPENDICES

Preface

1983 EDITION

When the manuscript of *Shared Fate* was sent to the publisher two decades ago I could not have foreseen so long a life for the book. I would like to think that it was in large part the merit of the work itself that kept it alive, but I am also aware of other forces that gave it support. The mid-nineteen sixties witnessed the rise of social movements that were concerned with many of the values which *Shared Fate* incorporated into a theory of adoptive relations. A new generation of social workers undoubtedly felt attracted to a theory that emphasized authentic and realistic definitions of adoptive parenthood over the more ambiguous definitions that had prevailed. Furthermore a generation of adopted persons was coming of age in a period that espoused the values of authenticity and realism. By the early 1970s the adoptee movement had taken off and it also discovered the Shared Fate theory of adoptive relations to fit its outlook and interests. Looking back I must therefore recognize that whatever intrinsic value *Shared Fate* had, it was helped to a long life by coincidental events in contemporary history.

In this second edition very little has been altered beyond the addition of a new preface and a postscript. When I tried, some years ago, to incorporate new and better statistical information to support the theory that was developed in this book, I discovered that I was unable to maintain the style and spirit of the 1964 book. I therefore decided to write a new book *(Adoptive Kinship)* in which the newer and better research-based statistics would be made public. The two books are interconnected. *Shared Fate* shows the development of the ideas that led to the theory of adoptive relations, while *Adoptive Kinship* takes the theory a step further. It does so not only by new research data but by showing that the problems so pervasive in adoptive parent-child relationships are not *sui generis,* are not of their participants' own making, but that they derive from the institutional arrangements which create and sustain adoptive kinship.

The subtitle no longer reads: 'a theory of adoption and mental health'. The book was never intended to bear it. My manuscript, as delivered to the publisher read: *Shared Fate—A Theory of Adoptive Relations.* An author is subjected to a great deal of editorial pressure, and some of it comes not from those concerned with content and style but from people who claim to know marketing. Well, shortly before the book went to press in 1963, someone in marketing got the idea that the subtitle I had chosen was not good for sales. It would have to be altered to make the book marketable. I recall that I was unhappy with it: what was meant by 'mental health'? And whose mental health was implied—the adoptive parents'?—the child's? But the process of the publishing machinery had gone too far. The author's objections were overridden. That is how *Shared Fate* appeared in 1964 with a subtitle I considered inappropriate if not misleading. Now, with a new edition being produced I am able to return to the theme of the original subtitle. However, the Shared Fate theory has now proved itself to be effective in the adoptive parent-child relationship. It has therefore seemed correct to think of Shared Fate as both a theory and a method of adoptive relationships.

In a preface the author is given leeway to speak personally. As I look back I recall some of the many communications concerning the book. Many of them came from social work professionals who commented on the beneficial effects they saw it have for changed attitudes within their agencies. But to my surprise and pleasure I also received support from adoptive parent associations. Eventually *Shared Fate* became the focus of what is sometimes called an 'invisible college', i.e. a group of people who correspond with each other around a technical problem, or a scientific thesis. Over the years I came to serve as informal mentor to dozens of graduate students and many working academics wrote to ask for my suggestions or critique. Such are some of the more delightful increments of one's work, far more important than the royalties that come from the publisher.

One such incremental event occurred under rather dramatic circumstances. Let me tell it here in some detail. It was a day in early May, 1979; I was in my office at the University of Waterloo, looking over my notes for that evening's first lecture on my new course 'The Sociology of Adoptive Kinship'. There was a knock on the door and the secretary brought in my mail. With it was a book parcel from South Africa. I could not recall having ordered anything from there for a long time. To my surprise I saw that I had been sent as a gift a small volume called *A Book of Life for an Adopted Child.*[1] With it came a letter by the author,[2] an adoptive mother. With her permission I am reproducing four paragraphs of her letter, for it shows how in one family the Shared Fate theory had become a method:

1. Avril and Martin Anderson (pseud.), *A Book of Life for an Adopted Child,* Cape Town, Howard Timmins, 1979

2. Her true name is Sharon Bacher; she has asked that I use it here.

> Dear Dr. Kirk,
>
> You will be surprised to be receiving this letter from me—a person you have never met or heard of. Nevertheless, I'm sure you will be gratified to know that your writings on adoption have been a source of inspiration to me, in far off South Africa.
>
> I am an adoptive mother who, in the last few years, has had to grapple with the dilemmas of adoptive parenthood, especially as these concern the task of 'telling' our daughter about her origins. It so happened that at this very time I was also studying for a degree in social work, and was inspired to read the adoption literature and write a dissertation in this field. In the course of my reading I found myself chasing up articles and writings by yourself.
>
> Your material provoked me, evoking at one and the same time a feeling of identification and strong denial. I was prepared to accept that adoptive parenting was unique. I could accept that we should be truthful and honest about ourselves as an adoptive family. But I balked against seeing or portraying our daughter's birth mother as a 'real' person.
>
> Your ideas continued to nag at me. But it was our daughter herself, who taught me (and my husband) the futility of our game for the fact was that she now knew she had another set of parents. And her deep need was to personalize these people. Did her mother give her a suitcase of clothes when she gave her to us? Did she also have blond hair? These were questions she asked, thus forcing us to acknowledge that this lady was indeed a strong and real presence in our family, and that she had come to stay.

The author's letter then continues to tell how these insights, coupled with the absence of a satisfactory literature for adopted children, led her to make up a book for her daughter. This personalized book was seen by friends, one of them a publisher, and that was how her book moved into print. As I read through her letter I became increasingly intrigued: how would one put the Shared Fate theory to use in a book for a pre-school child? Well, rather than saccharine and misleading statements like "she loved you so much that she gave you up for adoption," the book early-on discusses and shows simple pictures of human sex organs and the reproductive process. It is done in a family context, talking about mommies and daddies and little girls and boys. But it uses the exposition of reproduction to discuss both out-of-wedlock birth and infertility, the circumstances that, until quite recently, had given rise to the great majority of all adoptions between previously unrelated parties. Here was acknowledgement of difference in the context of the adopters telling their child. The book truly had taken my theory seriously and translated it into a dialogue between adoptive parent and young child. The author of *A Book of Life for an Adopted Child* says in the prefatory note: "A very special acknowledgement is due to Dr. H.D. Kirk, whose book *Shared Fate* provided the theoretical basis and a provoking stimulus for this book." Her words have encouraged me to think that even now, two decades after it first appeared, *Shared Fate* can serve as a guide to the intelligent adopter's family life.

Nevertheless, much has changed in the years since this book first appeared. It originated from information about families mainly constituted out of the twin problems of illegitimacy and infertility. But by the end of the 1960s the adoption picture in North America had begun to change. Manners and mores, accompanying the birth-control pill, had drastically altered, making for growing acceptance of unwed pregnancies. Fewer and fewer infants thus became available for adoption during the next decade. As a result, people anxious to adopt children have had to look to a reservoir previously regarded as less desirable: children from minority racial backgrounds at home or brought in from third world countries; children handicapped physically, mentally, or emotionally; finally older children as late as their teens have come to be candidates for adoption. What has further complicated the picture is the fact that among the adopters more and more are not infertile; many have had one or more children and are creating families not based on the deprivation of the infertile. With such changes in the structure and meaning of adoption, what can the Shared Fate theory and method contribute? Is it at all applicable to people in such greatly altered circumstances? In what sense can it be said that adopters of the older, the handicapped, or the racial minority child have need of the Shared Fate theory and method? Are such children not far more readily visible as not "home-made" than were the infants of the earlier wave of adoptions, often so carefully matched by appearance and background to the adopters? In other words, is it not understood that those who take a child of five or ten years old, or one with a limp or hard-of-hearing, or blind—that such people will as a matter of course acknowledge the facts of 'difference' so readily visible to their surroundings? On the face of it the insights of the Shared Fate theory need not be impressed on such adopters. I suspect that even a few years ago I would have given just such an answer. But more recent observation and information have taught me otherwise.

Here is what I now think: the process of wanting the child to become a member of their family apparently makes the adopters oblivious to the differences so obvious to outsiders. When the child is colored the adopters will become color-blind. When the child is physically or mentally handicapped the child will come to appear normal to them. And if the child enters their family past infancy, even if the child is already in school, and so brings a whole world of experiences and memories with him or her, the adoptive parents' enthusiasm may seek to cancel the child's past. While such kinds of 'myopia' may help the adopters in thinking of the child as their own, they also keep the new parents from recognizing the child's uniqueness and the reality of 'difference'.

Not long ago I met the director of an organization which is developing ways of placing older children into adoptive homes. This sensitive man pointed out that empathy and communication with the child in such circumstances require more than a willingness to think and feel oneself into the child's world. Often for empathy and communication to be meaningful they require specialized knowledge about the life circumstances of the particular child. For the child with a physical handicap there may be required special medical information. For the child from a minority ethnic or racial group the adopters may need to know about the way such people are seen and see themselves in the larger society. For the people who take an older child, say one in the first years of school, it becomes necessary to know something about the people and their life ways among whom the child has hitherto been living. Whether the change that the child is to undergo is to a different national or cultural milieu, the adopters must be able to grasp what this move implies for the child.

What these changed conditions of the past two decades tell us is that the Shared Fate theory and method continue to be applicable, but that they call for even greater attention by the professionals who help to arrange adoptions. It appears that the social services have in recent years become less interested in thorough preparation of adopters and children, than to find adoptive homes. The phenomenon of 'disrupted adoptions' having lately become professionally acknowledged[3] clearly calls for improved methods of preparing both parents and children for the difficulties to be expected and the tasks to be undertaken. If the principles of the Shared Fate theory are to hold true in the present they must be guides for making the educated guessing of the professionals more educated. To speak of 'educated guessing' is not derogatory: events are too swift to allow clinical workers to know with any degree of certainty how to fit their knowledge and their theories to drastically changing human life conditions. If the professionals are to be able to use this theory or any other in helping their clients make the best out of difficult circumstances, the professionals themselves must know the theory and its limitations as well as the pertinent parameters in the lives of these clients. This book is being reissued with a new preface and an added postscript in the hope that it will help in the training of a new generation of adoption workers.

3. "Adoption Disruptions", U.S. Department of Health and Human Services, Publication No. (OHDS) 81-30319, June 1981

In this context I want to acknowledge my regard for a growing group of researchers whose work has articulated with my own and who have made important contributions to the understanding of adoptive family relationships. Among these scholars I must mention at least the following: A.M. McWhinnie,[4] B. Jaffee and D. Fanshel,[5] M. Bohman,[6] J. Triseliotis,[7] A.D. Sorosky, A. Baran, and R. Pannor,[8] and W. Feigelman and A.R. Silverman.[9] This is not an exclusive list of useful sources, but I believe that these authors must be considered when in-service training is to be planned for social workers in child placement and post-adoption services.

While it is my hope that this new edition of *Shared Fate* will be found useful by a new generation of social workers, I mean it also to continue being a self-help tool for adoptive parents and for adult adopted persons who want to understand the world of their adoptive parents. As a self-help book it must, however, not be seen as a method encapsulated in a formula. As a self-help book it may serve as does a microscope which enlarges for us a field of vision ordinarily hidden from the naked eye. As we see this world of our own lives in the enlarged perspective of the Shared Fate theory we may be able to understand ourselves better as members of adoptive families, and understanding ourselves better, live more creatively.

Victoria, B.C.
December, 1983 — H. David Kirk

4. McWhinnie, *Adopted Children: How They Grow Up*, London: Routledge & Kegan Paul, 1967

5. Jaffee and Fanshel, *How They Fared in Adoption*, N.Y., Columbia U. Press, 1970

6. Bohman, *Adopted Children and Their Families*, Stockholm, Proprius, 1970

7. Triseliotis, *In Search of Origins*, London, Routledge & Kegan Paul, 1973

8. Sorosky, Baran, and Pannor, *The Adoption Triangle*, New York, Anchor, 1978

9. Feigelman and Silverman, *Chosen Children*, New York, Praeger, 1983

Preface
1963 EDITION

FOR the student of the family, adoption poses a number of theoretical questions. What functions does the practice have for the kinship system of the society in which it occurs? How far do the roles and relational norms of the adoptive family group coincide with, or depart from, those of the true family of procreation? How do the major cultural values that define the meanings of fertility and of parent-child relations affect the formation and development of adoptive families? This book has emerged from a series of studies designed to provide answers to such questions. In the course of the inquiry, new formulations evolved. It became evident that the cultural values within which adoptions are made are not consistently favorable to adoptive relations, and that adoptive parents are typically confronted with incongruous role obligations. Thus the findings indicated that adoptive relations are subject to particular strains. This recognition led us to investigate the parental means of coping with strain and consequences of different coping methods for the long-term prospects of the adoptive parent-child relationship.

With this focus the investigation assumed relevance for practitioners in social work and in psychological services to children and families. Such practitioners are involved in the selection of parents for children, in preparing novices for adoptive parental roles, and in counseling members of adoptive families. Any light from nonclinical sources that could be shed on the processes of adoptive relations should enhance the effectiveness of those in clinical practice. As the book's subtitle indicates, this is a suggestive work culminating in a theory of adoptive relations and not a handbook with neat guidelines for practice. Admittedly practitioners must act in the immediacy; they can seldom defer making decisions because they are without definitive knowledge. But it is my hope that this book will help practitioners to make their educated guesses more educated and to utilize the wealth of their clinical experience in the testing of relevant theories. *Exceptio regulam probat* does not mean that the exception proves, but that it probes or tests the rule, the model, the theory.

This book could not have come into being without the cooperation of more than 2,000 couples who are adoptive parents. Again and again their interest and their insights redefined the problem and suggested new avenues for the conduct of the inquiry. Evidence of this will be found throughout these pages. Similarly, much has been learned from contact with adopted children. Their penetrating questions and perceptions are capable of silencing some glib adult formulations of reality, as illustrated, for example, by this poignant statement from an eleven-year-old adopted boy: "The child who is born into his family is like a board that's nailed down from the start. But the adopted child, him the parents have to nail down, otherwise he is like a loose board in mid-air." This statement identifies the position of the adoptee as achieved, whereas that of the child born into his family is ascribed. It also points to a special requirement for the role of the adoptive parent. To these instructors, adopted children and adoptive parents, I am greatly indebted.

Most of the adoptive parents participating in the studies on which this book is based were reached through the good offices of several social agencies and associations of adoptive parents. Thanks are due these organizations, their boards, and executives: The Child and Family Service, Elmira, N.Y.; The Spence-Chapin Adoption Service,* New York City; Children's Services, Cleveland, Ohio; The State of California Department of Social Welfare, Sacramento; The Los Angeles County Bureau of Adoptions; The Catholic Children's Aid Society, Toronto; The Children's Aid Society of Metropolitan Toronto; The Children's Service Centre, Montreal; The Barker Foundation, Washington, D.C.; The Adopted Children's Association of Whittier; The Adopted Children's Association of Los Angeles; and the Adoptive Parents Committee of New York.

Over the years so many people have made contributions to the work which led to this book that it would be quite impossible to name them all. Most of them, like my former teachers and my research assistants, I must thank collectively. Some I would like to mention specifically: Lee and Evelyn Brooks, whose work on adoption (1939) was a major pioneering effort, and Mrs. Muriel B. McCrea, Executive Director of the Children's Service Centre, Montreal, have over the years consistently encouraged my work; several members of her staff, especially Miss Alice Westcott, have been of great assistance. Mrs. Marie Roberts valiantly performed many necessary but unrewarding chores in the early stages of the research, and Mrs. Florence Fyfe indulgently typed and retyped the manuscript at her multipurpose kitchen table. Mr. Thomas Simpson and Mrs. Aline Pick Kessler of The Free Press have greatly helped by their cogent editorial critique. My friends Malcolm Farmer, Duncan Mitchell, and Charles Browning helped, in the course of many conversations, to clarify ideas

* This applies to the agency under the direction of Miss Dorothea P. Coe and Miss Roberta Andrews.

which found their way into this book. But the greatest debt of gratitude is owed to my wife, Ruth Vail Kirk, for her candid appraisal of her role as adoptive mother and for her active participation in several phases of the research. Her sensitive analysis of data frequently made the difference between banal and thought-provoking interpretation.

Financial assistance has been received from the McGill University Research Fund; the Harry M. Cassidy Memorial Fund; the Department of National Health and Welfare; The National Institute of Mental Health, United States Public Health Service; and the Mental Hygiene Institute, Montreal. Their support has been indispensable and has been much appreciated.

I am greatly indebted to the adoptive parents who have allowed me to quote from their letters and to the publishers and editors who have given their permission to reprint from their publications. In each case, the book, journal, author, and publisher are identified in the bibliography.

Although a great many persons have had a hand in making this book possible, the responsibility for its contents is of course solely mine. In spite of whatever shortcomings it might possess, I hope that it will add to our understanding of the phenomenon we call the family, and that it will be of some practical use to adoptive parents and children.

H. DAVID KIRK

Montreal, Canada
May, 1963

Overview

Studies in the Adoption Research Project

Date of Study	*Type of Study and Methods*	*Reports*
1951-1953	Community Attitudes impinging on adoptive families, Public opinion study; interviews with 183 householders in upstate New York community.	H. D. Kirk, *Community Sentiments in Relation to Child Adoption,* Unpublished Ph.D. thesis, Cornell University, 1953.
1952-1953	Content analysis of professional literature as indicators of values likely to influence public and adopters.	H. D. Kirk, "Values Related to Adoption—An Aspect of the Child's Heritage," Paper read to section of National Conference on Adoption (Child Welfare League of America), 1955.
1952-1953	Mail questionnaire study of 97 adoptive couples. Interest in their self attitudes and experiences with attitudes of others.	
1955-1960	Survey of self-attitudes and experiences of 1,532 adoptive parents. Mail questionnaire instrument, sent to adopters in Quebec, Ontario, New York, Ohio, and California. Analysis of characteristics of non-	Kornbluth *et al., Some Aspects of What Is Important to Adoptive Parents,* MSW Group Thesis, McGill University, School of Social Work, 1957. Cynberg *et al. Insights into*

	respondents of the mail questionnaire.	*Adoption,* MSW Group Thesis, McGill University, School of Social Work, 1958. H. D. Kirk, "A Dilemma of Adoptive Parenthood: Incongruous Role Obligations," *Marriage and Family Living,* XXI, No. 4 (1959), 316-326.
1956-1957	Replication of New York Public opinion study of 1952, for samples of English and French householders in Quebec.	Bramble *et al., An Exploration into Some of the Attitudes in the Community Surrounding the Adoptive Family,* MSW Group Thesis, McGill University, School of Social Work, 1957.
1957-1958	Intensive interviews with 70 adoptive parents who had previously replied to the mail questionnaire of 1956. Use of interview schedule.	Bedoukian *et al., Adaptation to Adoptive Parenthood,* MSW Group Thesis, McGill University, School of Social Work, 1958.
1959-1961	Adaptations to Role Handicap in Adoptive Family Life. Studies of three associations of adoptive parents in California to identify the functions of association membership.	H. D. Kirk, *Parent-Child Relations in Adoption,* Six Lectures (mimeographed), McGill University, School of Social Work, 1961.
	Content analysis of 184 letters to the editor of a woman's magazine answer to article: "To My Adopted Daughter—I Wish I Hadn't Told You."	H. D. Kirk, "Guarding the Ramparts—Reader Reactions to a Magazine Article Questioning a Social Work Prescription," *The Social Worker* (June-July, 1962), 31-43.
	Preparation of self-administered questionnaire subsequently pretested with 45 couples and ultimately completed by 283 couples.	H. D. Kirk, "Nonfecund People as Parents," *Fertility and Sterility,* XIV, No. 3 (1963), 310-319.
1962-1963	Survey of clinics, youth shelters, and hospitals in Montreal to determine proportion of adoptees in the child population of their clients.	H.D. Kirk, K. Jonassohn, and A.D. Fish, "Are Adopted Children more Vulnerable to Stress?" *Archives of General Psychiatry,* Vol. 14, March 1966.
1963-1968	Study of family structure and the health of children. Normal population sample of 2,300 children in Nova Scotia, allowing for comparisons by age, gender, and birth/adoptive status.	H.D. Kirk and K. Jonassohn, *Halifax Children,* A Statistical Report. University of Waterloo, 1973.

Shared Fate

CHAPTER ONE

*

Adoptive Relations in the Making

*

IN modern industrial societies, adoption is practiced as an emergency measure. Courts and agencies generally take the view that the original family relationship should be preserved for the child whenever possible. The practice is thus encircled by protective steps that signify the official reluctance to tamper with bonds of consanguinity. This orientation is in marked contrast to that in primitive societies (Lowie, 1930), particularly the recorded instances of adoption in the arctic (Boas, 1888), Polynesia (Firth, 1936), and Micronesia (Weckler, 1953).

Where adoption is viewed as an emergency act, it should be resorted to relatively infrequently. Considering the total stream of family behavior, the phenomenon of adoption is indeed numerically rather insigificant. The best available evidence suggests that about 2.5 per cent of the child population of the United States is adopted.[1]

This book makes a further reduction in numbers. We shall address ourselves exclusively to those situations in which no kinship ties existed between adopters and adopted before adoption. It has been estimated that approximately half of all the adoptions made in the United States since 1943 are of this type. Our neglect of adoptions by relatives and our concentration on adoptions by nonrelatives stems from the fact that in the latter type the problem of our study can be stated and identified more clearly than in the former. In the case of adoptions by couples, especially the involuntarily childless, who take children to whom they previously have had no kinship ties, the circumstances of deprivation for both parents and children are more clearly marked than in adoptions by relatives. This chapter will deal principally with the deprivations that are involved in childlessness and in a childless couple's attempts at adopting.

In a recent study of adoptive family life,[2] 283 couples, most of whom had been childless prior to adoption, were asked: "There was once a time in your life when you wanted children but could not have them. What word or words would best describe your feelings at that time?" Husbands and wives received separate but identical questionnaires. The following answers are typical of the total group; the replies from a particular couple have here been placed side by side.

These examples show that involuntary childlessness represents a serious crisis for women. The terms used by wives have

1. This figure is based on the ratio between the estimated number of annual adoption petitions granted by U.S. Courts (Children's Bureau, 1962) and the annual number of births in the United States (*Health, Education, and Welfare Trends*, 1962). Such a ratio is only roughly indicative of the number of adopted children in the child population. The statistical bases for an accurate adoption rate are currently not available.

2. See pp. xi-xii, Overview of Studies in the Adoption Research Project, 1959-1961.

an emergency quality about them. Men, although they may be disappointed by childlessness, appear to feel less deprived. However real their loss, it is probably more readily compensated for by occupational activity.

Wife		*Husband*
Despair and bitterness	—	Disappointed
Disappointed, at times desperate feeling of hopelessness and inferiority	—	Concern about wife's reactions
Frustration and disappointment; I had always assumed that I would have children and eagerly anticipated family life	—	Disappointment, but largely because of wife's feelings
Forlorn, unfulfilled, lost	—	Never felt this way
Uselessness	—	Disappointed
Unhappy, depressed	—	(no answer)
Utter desolation and despair	—	(no answer)
Depressed, heartbroken	—	Incomplete
Bitterness, longing	—	Disappointment
I think it was my biggest disappointment. I was completely miserable	—	Disheartened
Not a whole woman—heartbroken—then realizing that I must cope with and deal with this given situation	—	Anxiety
Absolutely heartsick	—	Disappointed
Frustration	—	Deep disappointment
A terrific desire for children and a *desolate fear* that we might not have any	—	Inadequate
Frustrated, depressed	—	Did not give up hope
Sadness	—	(no answer)
Disappointment, feeling a flop as a wife and woman	—	Regret
Completely lost	—	Frustrated; also feeling I had failed my wife
Misery	—	(no answer)
Yearning	—	(no answer)
Bitterness and self-pity	—	(no answer)

The simple demonstration of the spouses' relative deprivation was supplemented by an analysis of the terms used to express deprivation. These were sorted into categories of "strong," "medium," and "weak." The brief listing below will suggest how the degree of deprivation was assessed in the terms used.

Degrees of Deprivation

Strong	*Medium*	*Weak*
Great bitterness and self-pity	Frustrated	Disappointed until found out about adoption
Very unhappy	Depressed	
Terrific desire for children and desolate fear that we might not have any	Wanted children, disappointed at not having them	
Concerned—afraid of giving wife inadequate, unsatisfactory experience	Concerned about wife's reactions	

In a total of 434 classifiable replies (the sum of husbands' and wives' responses), 149 (34 per cent) had characteristics of strong deprivation. Out of 241 wives, 42 per cent expressed their deprivation in "strong" terms, while only 24 per cent of 193 husbands' replies could be so classified. These figures once again suggest that women are more vulnerable than men to the deprivation of childlessness. In spite of this insight, we shall for the present refrain from a systematic differentiation of the spouses' deprivation. Our current task consists of identifying the specific aspects of deprivation experienced by the childless couple who move toward adoption.

For the pursuit of this and subsequent analyses, we shall need a minimum of technical language. This minimum is made palatable by the fact that sociologists have made use of some of the language of the theatre, particularly in the concept of "social role." Around it has arisen a mode of describing and analyzing human relationships (Sarbin, 1954). One imaginative writer has recently shown a way of using the full range of dramaturgical ideas in an attempt at understanding the human personality (Goffman, 1959). This approach of dramatic imagery will permit us to move directly into our context which is the adoptive relationship.

Let us conceive of the main activities of human life as actions in a play in which the actors play a series of roles. In that drama there are, most commonly, the roles of male and female; childhood, youth, maturity, and old age; father, mother, and child; health and sickness; and the whole range of our occupations. As on the stage, we, the actors in the real life drama, require some degree of competence. Let us briefly identify what training this requires. The role to be played must be relatively well described. Thus, for fatherhood there must be a script to suggest what minimum it takes to be a father, as well as what it takes to be a *good* father. Such a script exists, of course, only partially in print. Occasionally the laws have something to say about our roles, as in the case of a parent's rights and responsibilities. But these legal definitions in themselves could hardly tell a person how to enact the role of father or mother successfully. This is learned from early childhood on, and from association with fathers and mothers, one's own and those of one's peers. A person gradually acquires a picture of what the people around him, especially the people in his immediate circle, mean by a "good father." Overt acts and sentiments, gestures and words—in sum, the total behavior of our contemporaries—provide each of us with the basic script from which we derive our knowledge of certain common roles.

We shall now compare and contrast the role script for parenthood in our culture with the actual situation in which involuntarily childless couples find themselves. This listing will highlight the fact that the nonfecund couple moving into adoption is deprived and that their deprivation is not simply one of children but, more properly, the lack of an appropriate cultural script.

ROLE PREPARATION

Preparation for adult life presumes that there will be children. This implies that persons moving into marriage ordinarily take for granted their potential fertility. This mental link between marriage and fertility is illustrated in the advice given to parents in a publication on the sex education of children (Child Study Association, 1954, 14). Under "First Questions," we find the child asking, "Will I Have a Baby Too?"

> Most children ask this or assume it with a flat statement that they intend to have babies when they grow up. You can agree that they will be parents without going into the complicated ideas of marriage and adult love relationships. *Simply tell them "when you grow up you'll get married and have babies."* Small boys, of course, should not be allowed to think that they can bear babies, but are generally satisfied to know they will be daddies, even before they have thought to ask what a daddy's role is. (Emphasis added.)

Note that the ability to have babies is presupposed here. This ability is made clear to mean "bearing" when the book differentiates between little girls and boys. Although the cultural script prepares people for fertility, there is little, if any, preparation for sterility and its consequences. Thus, under the heading of "Teenage Questions," the sex education manual of the Child Study Association briefly defines the term sterility, but it does not apply the facts of sterility to the role training for adulthood. In an interview study of 70 adoptive parents,[3] it was found that in only nine of the 70 cases could a spouse recall ever having considered the possibility of sterility or other causes of nonfecundity before it actually faced them as a marital problem.

The vast majority of people have lived with their own parents during part of their youth and are aware of models for parenthood that fit the circumstances of fecundity. But adoptive parents have in most instances had little or no intimate contact with adopters *as adoptive parents,* or for that matter, with other adopted persons. Their preparation for parenthood derives from *biological* parents.

Preparation for parental roles, especially the mother role, is assisted by early childhood play. During courtship and early

3. See p. xii, Overview of Studies in the Adoption Research Project, 1957-1958.

marriage, aided by the assumption of potential fertility, the couple recall their experiences during discussions of what they will do when their own first child comes. Their hopes and plans are partly cast in terms of their own experience. The pre-adoptive couple, however, will find that their recall is not fully suited to the preparation for the experience of "substitute" parenthood.

Preparation for biological parenthood and parental roles is gradual—the period of pregnancy provides the couple with a known timetable that moves them imperceptibly toward progressive involvement in their coming parental tasks. In contrast, preparation for adoptive parenthood tends to be abrupt with no clearcut timetable by which the couple can shape their feelings and thoughts about their hoped-for parenthood. This uncertainty is somewhat mitigated in agency adoptions because there comes a point at which the agency lets the applicants know that they are accepted (perhaps comparable to the medical test of conception). However, there is seldom a timetable for would-be adoptive parents that assures them of parenthood in so many months.

Maternity clothing is worn about the midterm of pregnancy. The clothing is an external sign to others of one's changing position, and thus one enters already upon the path of developing parenthood. The folklore about irrational food cravings suggests that the culture gives wide latitude to the pregnant woman's concern for herself. In adoption there are few signs useful to oneself or to others for underscoring the changing status which is being anticipated and worked for. Perhaps the fact that the couple have passed an agency's eligibility requirements may serve as such a sign, as exemplified in the following account of a somewhat pointed discussion an adoptive mother held with a sister-in-law who was particularly fecund. This sister-in-law had made a remark suggesting that the adoptive mother could not know certain things because she had not produced her own children. The adoptive mother retorted proudly,

"All you had to do was to go to bed; we had to prove to some pretty particular inspectors our fitness for being parents."

ROLE AUTONOMY

The biological parents are, ultimately, independent in the procurement of their child. However much they may utilize the technological services of medicine, surgery, and hospital, they know that procurement is possible without all these services. Essentially they are not in need of a "middle man." This autonomy is in line with the value system of the middle class, which emphasizes the importance of independence. On the other hand, adoptive couples, who are typically recruited from middle- and upper-middle class groups, are ultimately dependent on the services of a middle man, whether this helper is professional or not, be he friend, social worker, physician, lawyer, minister, or black marketeer. This dependence tends to be increased in agency adoptions, which preclude direct transactions between natural and adoptive parents. In a more subtle sense, agency adoptions tend to make the adoptive applicants dependent because there is seldom an overt listing of the agency's criteria for the evaluation of applicants and their eligibility. This dependence has been dramatically illustrated by Cady (1952, 33-34). He described an interview which he and his wife had with the social worker:

> The session then developed into a casual but searching probe of our motives for wanting to take a little girl; what we thought we could do to make her happy; the temperament of our son; our preferences in amusement and recreation; our religious life and affiliation, and our ideas about child training. Glancing at Betsy during the inquisition, I was amused, anxious as I was, to note that she wore a look of mingled deference, hope, and apprehension —a strangely familiar look. At first I couldn't identify it. Then I remembered where I had often seen it—on the faces of penitentiary prisoners at the parole hearings that would decide their future. I imagine I didn't look much different myself.

The biological tasks of gestation are entirely those of the female and this "divison of labor" aids later solidification of husband-wife roles. Division of labor makes for interdependence and therefore leads to social solidarity. In the preparation for adoptive parenthood, man and woman have biologically inactive roles, both spouses having a role similar to that of the male in the biological situation. This state therefore precludes ready role differentiation. We should expect the greater difficulties among relatively traditional couples where role differentiation between husband and wife is typically rather pronounced and where there is usually less emphasis on companionship.

At the birth of their first child, parents are typically in their twenties, the wife in her early twenties. It has been estimated that in the early 1950's a majority of married women had concluded their childbearing by the time they were twenty-six years old (Glick, 1957). Further, the time between marriage and the birth of the first child is typically rather short (*i.e.*, between one and two and a half years). Both these factors, the spouses' ages and the length of their marriage at the birth of their first child, may be considered in favor of relatively easy transition to the changes which life with an infant implies. That is, the couple is likely to be still rather flexible for learning the tasks of child care and their married-pair life patterns have not as yet solidified so far as to make the new parental activities difficult. Whereas the adopting parents are typically 7-8 years older than their biological counterparts when their first child comes. Furthermore, there is a wider age range for adopting than for natural parents, (*i.e.*, at the time of the arrival of the first child, there are proportionately far more adopting parents over forty years than natural parents). This, plus the fact that they have had a long and frequently frustrating time between marriage and adoption, implies that the shift to parenthood will involve greater difficulties for adoptive parents than for natural parents. One might also want to consider the simple fact that people in their twenties typically have physical energies for the twenty-four-hour round of chores which infant care presupposes, while people in their thirties may have a somewhat lower level of energy to expend.

ROLE OBLIGATIONS

Because parental obligations are total and unqualified, parents are expected to be accepting of all deficiencies in their offspring. This obligation of unqualified acceptance means that one is not allowed to be preferential, but that every child is desirable and a proper member "for better or for worse," and that he is so permanently. Adopting parents, in contrast, are apparently expected to be qualified in the feeling-connection they make with the child during the period before legal adoption. The adopting parents know that there is at least a possibility that they will not be accepted in the end, or that for some other reason the child may not be theirs to keep. This knowledge may stop some from giving themselves to the child as completely and unqualifiedly as they otherwise would. There is still a further factor which reinforces the uncertainty of their parental relationship at that time. Some of the people who have given information have said that they felt upset when doctor or agency counseled them to return a child found to be physically or otherwise defective. Such rationality and qualified relationhip are clearly not applicable to parenthood as we know it, and such suggestions are likely to leave the adopting couple at a loss as to the meaning of their status. This element of rationality, as an expectation of adoptive parenthood, is reflected in laws providing for the possibility that an adoption, once legalized, can be terminated.

SANCTIONS AND REWARDS FOR ROLE PERFORMANCE

Once the couple is licensed to marry, biological parenthood has no further requirements. In agency adoptions, however, and to a lesser degree in independent adoptions, the adopting couple must show their eligibility for the parental status they seek. They must provide sufficient evidence of psychological stability, a stable marital relationship, economic stability, and, in some cases, religious membership as well. It should also be noted that this examination of their suitability for parenthood comes at a time in their lives when they have long been frustrated, and feel discouraged, so that they may find this test especially distasteful.

Parental status is initiated during pregnancy and fully secured at birth. All rights, duties, and privileges of parenthood accrue to the new parents at that time. This fact aids them in directing all their feelings to the infant as a *member* of their family unit. Parental status is not fully secured at the arrival of the child in the adoptive household. Adopting parents are responsible for the child's maintenance and safety, but guardianship rights remain in the hands of others who are still *in loco parentis* (*i.e.*, either the natural parent(s) or the agency). (Note here that an interlocutory decree of adoption aids the adopters by giving them some official assurance that their present quasi-host status is only temporary and will most likely be transformed into a full parental status in due course.)

The relative certainty of a child's coming in the biological situation makes possible an early sharing of the news with the couple's parents. This can be expected to lead to considerable support from the family. The rejoicing of parents and in-laws is an aid through some of the trying times which may be part of the pregnancy. The considerable uncertainty connected with adoption plans frequently inhibits sharing plans with members of the wider family. Thus, there is the additional disadvantage that the family, through ignorance, may be unable to rally around and support them in this difficult period.

At the time of a child's birth, the family usually gathers around the new parent couple, looking for family likenesses in the newborn, remarking on the choice of name, and they frequently participate in religious ceremonies, whereby the baby's membership in the group is asserted. In adoption, there are no ceremonies of this order to mark the new member's arrival in the family. Knowledge of the rupture of the family line precludes looking for family likenesses.

In our society, biological parenthood is sanctioned and rewarded by a variety of benefits which are conferred on the new parents. For instance, medical and hospital care plans recognize and help pay for certain costs involved in the child's arrival. Further, Federal and state or provincial tax laws allow medical costs of pregnancy and birth to be deducted from taxable income. For adopting couples, there is no equivalent arrangement to take care of the costs of the child's arrival. Tax laws do not uniformly make provision for the deduction of expenses involved in adoption. Thus, while California income-tax law permits such expenses as legitimate deductions, Federal law does not do so. (In 1960, California Congressman Kasem sought unsuccessfully to introduce such a bill: HR 9333.)

If the child dies, even shortly after birth, the natural parents are given the support of understanding and sympathy of their friends and the community, just as they would over the death of a family member of longer standing. But when an adoptive couple loses a child prior to legalization, either by death or by removal and return to the natural parent, there is no great likelihood that they will receive an equivalent support from others. This is illustrated by the experience of a family which encountered the removal from their household of a child who had been with them for over a year but had not yet become legally theirs; they encountered this belated response from a friendly neighbor: "I felt deeply with you but didn't let you know because I did not know what to say."

This comparison of circumstances associated with family formation, biological and adoptive, emphasizes important differences between the two means of parenthood. It makes clear that the phase of preparation for adoptive parenthood is accompanied by events which involve more or less severe deprivations, the lack of elements normally presupposed for marriage, and the cultural script that goes with it.

Let us now consider what this discrepancy between the expected and the actually encountered forces means for an actor. As long as the situation he meets is at least similar to that for which the script prepared him, he has a good chance to be competent in the performance of his role. But when the actual situation of the drama is quite different from the one which the script led him to expect, the likelihood of the actor's competent role performance is, of necessity, greatly reduced. Only a very alert and inventive actor can adequately deal with such a suddenly and radically changed situation.

Discrepancies between the cultural script and the personal or group encounter with reality are illustrated by sudden serious illness, severe accidents, bereavement, and by natural and man-made disasters which destroy life and property. "Situational discrepancies" are by no means uncommon; but because of men's dependence on one or another cultural script which regulates their expectations, the discrepancies always produce more or less serious social dislocations. In terms of social relationships, situational discrepancies tend to result in interference with competent role performance. They lead to "role handicap." Bereavement, for instance, involves role handicap, in that the bereaved can no longer engage in their accustomed or wished-for relationship with the dead person, and in disasters one may be prevented from carrying out important role obligations. Eventually, of course, the situation tends to become "normalized," which only means that a different script has been substituted for the original one which no longer fits the situation. Role handicap is thus reduced through a variety of means of adaptation. To a population at peace, the sudden death of many children, as for instance in a schoolhouse disaster, is "unthinkable," whereas to a population accustomed to war conditions, events with similar consequences become "thinkable." There the participants learn to act on the basis of a modified or drastically altered script.

Situational discrepancies have interpersonal concomitants. We observe four types of role handicap, resulting from discrepancies which interfere with role clarity, with role autonomy, with role obligations, and with sanctions and rewards. Several of these objective social factors of role handicap have corresponding subjective states which have been described as *alienation*. Thus, lack of role clarity implies that the individual has a problem in "understanding the events in which he is engaged," a type of alienation that Seeman (1959, 786) calls "meaninglessness." A lack of role autonomy implies that the individual will expect "that his own behavior cannot determine the occurrence of the outcomes, or reinforcements, he seeks." This is Seeman's "powerlessness" (1959, 784). Obstacles to the performance of role obligations are likely to lead the individual to expect that "socially unapproved behaviors are required to achieve given goals." Seeman calls this type of alienation "normlessness" (1959, 787-788).

Depending on the degree of an actor's role handicap, his sense of alienation should be more or less severe. As we have already seen, the deprivation of childlessness is reported in more drastic terms by women than by men. Now we shall come to see that women also report more instances of role handicap resulting from the adoption process. In the 1961 questionnaire study of 283 adoptive couples, the spouses were separately asked:

> Looking back over some of the experiences you had in becoming an adoptive parent, which of the following experiences did you at the time find rather difficult or hard, and which not so difficult or hard?[4]
>
> —Learning that you would probably not have a child born to you.

4. Respondents were also asked to specify when an experience item did not apply in their case and show why it did not apply.

—Having to depend on the assistance of outsiders (agency, doctor) in getting a child.

—Having to furnish a medical certificate to prove to an agency that you could not have children born to you.

—Having to prove to the authorities (agency and/or court) that you were suitable for raising children, something biological parents don't have to prove.

—Having no dependable timetable (such as a nine-month pregnancy) for knowing how soon the child would arrive.

—Knowing, that even when the child came to you, and until legal adoption, you would not be full parents.

—Being informed that you should tell the child of the adoption.

—Discovering that among your family and friends there are those who are ill-informed about the meaning of being an adoptive parent.

This question was analyzed in part by a comparison of the frequencies with which men and women mentioned the difficulties they had encountered. Fifty-four per cent of the wives and 30 per cent of the husbands said they found the experience of childlessness difficult. Thirty-eight per cent of the wives and 24 per cent of the husbands deplored the lack of a timetable in family formation by adoption. Thirty-one per cent of the wives and 20 per cent of the husbands mentioned three or more difficulties. Nineteen per cent of the wives and 32 per cent of the husbands claimed to have found none of the listed experiences difficult or hard.

In this chapter we have investigated the cultural and social meanings of childlessness, and of the first steps into adoptive parenthood. In the following chapter we shall look at certain common conditions that highlight and thus tend to reinforce the role handicap associated with the initial phases of adoptive relations.

CHAPTER TWO

*

The Pervading Environment

*

CULTURAL scripts, like those for stage plays, have to be learned. Such learning makes an actor not only sensitive to specific cues related to the part he is to play, but also ready to ignore other stimuli which are not articulated with his role. When, in the midst of a performance, there occurs an unexpected event which threatens to disrupt things, it takes especially alert and inventive actors to keep the action going. The script and directions which have hitherto guided the actor are no longer reliable. He is on his own. At first, he is likely to operate by trial and error, selecting from the various stimuli around him those that appear most appropriate in his current situation. His problem is to learn the identity of the stimuli which will make his role effective under the changed circumstances.

As we saw in the previous chapter, the involuntarily childless seldom have any preparation for the drastic change in life expectation which childlessness brings with it. They too must begin to "play it by ear," depending on whatever stimuli are available to them. And they are by no means without such cues to the way they must now remake their picture of themselves and the part they might yet play in the drama of marriage and family. The cues which are available are rather diffuse, deriving from the feelings and beliefs, values and attitudes—the "sentiments" of the other actors and of the audience.

In this chapter, we shall investigate the environment of sentiments from which the adopters are likely to select the cues for "keeping going." From the possible fellow-actors we have chosen two groups which seem particularly pertinent: the couple's parents and the social work practitioners. The audience consists of other people outside the family—friends and acquaintances—whose outlook impinges on the adopting couple and which partially defines their situation. In a way, the adopters themselves belong to this audience. They adopt almost invariably as a last resort; at the start of marriage and the contemplation of parenthood nothing could ordinarily be further from their minds. But people who do not think of themselves as candidates for a particular position are not as likely to be protective of its good reputation as are people who expect to be incumbents in it. The recently married are therefore likely to harbor essentially the same feelings about substitute parenthood as are current in the community at large. Only when childlessness appears to be their own lot will they be forced to look more closely at this body of sentiments and take some personal stand. If they move toward substitute parenthood they will probably make modifications in their attitudes. In trying to make this shift, the couple may be quite successful, but older attitudes will never be entirely absent. Like cues learned early, and often responded to, they are well entrenched in the memory and the emotions.

In a community like Mokil (Weckler, 1953), where adoption is an everyday matter, commonly understood and sanctioned, adopters will have little if anything to alter in their previous viewpoint. In North America and perhaps even more in some European societies, adoption is less typical and less clearly sanctioned, a more peculiar and problematic event. In the sense that the adopters are part of that society in which they live, we have here called them part of the audience; in the sense that the adopters have most likely shared popular sentiments, we have called this chapter The Pervading Environment. Obviously, we cannot study this environment as it was in the adopters before they adopted. To learn about it, we must turn to persons who represent significant carriers of relevant sentiments.

ATTITUDES OF THE ADOPTERS' PARENTS

When the spouses first think about adoption they confront a special set of persons whose opinions they probably regard as relatively important. Among these sentiment carriers are their own parents, the potential grandparents. We are not suggesting that the spouses contemplating adoption would ask their parents for advice or consent. Rather, their parents represent important reference points, since they achieved what the adopters were unable to achieve. The adopters are therefore likely to feel less capable, less adequate, in comparison with their own parents from whom they have gained their most powerful image of the meaning of fecundity and parenthood. The couple contemplating adoption is thus probably sensitive to the way their parents overtly or covertly regard adoption. Out of 1,532 couples who took part in the mail questionnaire study of 1956,[1] 60 per cent had three or more parents living and 88 per cent had at least two. Inquiry about the attitudes of the adopters' parents was made in two questions. The first asked about the way the parents had reacted to the couple's adoption plans. The second question asked about their attitudes after the child had come.

1. See p. xi, Overview of Studies in the Adoption Research Project, 1955-1958.

Table 1 shows the degree of grandparental approval before and after the child's arrival.

Table 1
Numbers of Adopters' Parents Whose Attitudes toward the First Adoption Were Reported, and Their Degree of Approval Before and After the Child Came into the Home (in Per Cent)*

	HUSBANDS' PARENTS				*WIVES' PARENTS*			
	Fathers		*Mothers*		*Fathers*		*Mothers*	
	N	*%*	*N*	*%*	*N*	*%*	*N*	*%*
Before the child came	(907)	72	(1150)	76	(979)	80	(1199)	86
After the child came†	(907)	95	(1165)	96	(978)	97	(1212)	98

* The significance of differences between percentages in this and subsequent tables, and in prose accounts, was calculated either by chi-square tests or by reference to tables prepared by Davies (1951). Unless otherwise noted, the differences are significant at the .05 level or better.
† The differences between percentages in this row are not significant at the .05 level.

Although the large majority of the adopters' parents approved before as well as after adoption, there was an almost complete swing to approval once the child had become part of the adoptive household. In the period before the child came, the wife's parents were more prone to approve than were the husband's parents and potential grandmothers on both sides of the family were more accepting than grandfathers.

When we ask ourselves why potential grandparents should hesitate at all in giving their full approval to adoption, it occurs to us that the attitudes held by parents of *childless* couples differ from those held by the parents of *fecund* couples. Table 2 shows how fathers of nonfecund and of fecund adopters reacted to their children's plans for adoption.

Table 2
Reported Rate of Approval of the First Adoption Plans by the Couple's Fathers

Couple's State of Fecundity at Time Adoption Plans Made	*Husband's Father*		*Wife's Father*	
	N	*%*	*N*	*%*
Childless couples*	(753)	75	(829)	79
Couples having at least one child born to them	(135)	57	(140)	69

* The difference between percentages in this row is not significant at the .05 level.

The rate of paternal approval is substantially smaller for the adoption plans of couples who have children of their own than it is for those who are childless. This suggests that a significant minority of husbands' fathers represent, so to speak, guardians of the blood line, readier to look favorably on adoption by the childless than by the fecund. Whether these attitudes derive from concern with the protection of "heirs of the body," or from fear that a mixed (biological and adoptive) family will present unnecessary psychological difficulties, we cannot tell from these data.

In the light of the discussion in the first chapter, which introduced the idea of role handicap derived from nonfecundity, we have now found that such negative attitudes displayed by potential grandparents seem to stem from sentiments emphasizing fecundity. If we assume that such sentiments are widespread, the larger proportion of approval can be viewed as an act of pity and consolation rather than of enthusiastic consensus. This idea is supported by unsolicited information obtained from adoptive mothers. One had informed her parents that she and her husband were planning to adopt because she was found to be sterile. She subsequently had a reply from her mother, approving of the plans for adoption, but adding these tell-tale words: "Don't worry—Dad and I love you anyhow." Another woman, whose parents-in-law are of Latin American origin, reports that the adopted grandchildren "are not mistreated by the grandparents—they are just not loved like the other children. There are other children who are idolized. One of these was born out of wedlock. One was the cause of a forced marriage." This adoptive mother has a history of frequent illness. At such times her mother-in-law has said to her son, apparently in jest, "Why don't you trade her in for a new model?"

In a small group meeting of adoptive couples, the conversation turned to the attitudes of the grandparents. Those present indicated that, although their parents had raised no objections to their plans to adopt, several showed a decided lack of enthusiasm for it. One woman, the oldest of three daughters, reminisced that her adopted son was the first grandchild for her parents. To all appearances they were very pleased with the child. But when one of her younger sisters subsequently became pregnant, the baby crib which had been in the family for several generations, and in which the three girls had also slept, was given to the couple expecting this baby. Events such as these indicate that the adopters' parents may harbor sentiments that emphasize fecundity even when their overt attitudes are accepting of adoption.

The more covert sentiments, which this analysis has shown to exist among adopters' parents, are undoubtedly not lost on the adopters themselves. If they are trying to reorient themselves away from fecundity values and toward the dignity of substitute parental roles, then the emphasis on fecundity on the part of fellow-actors who are close to them is bound to make their task more difficult.

SOME ASPECTS OF THE ATTITUDES OF THE SOCIAL WORK PROFESSION

A second set of people whose attitudes and views of adoption become crucial to adoptive parents are the professionals who are instrumental in the making of many adoptions. The United States Children's Bureau estimate for 1960 indicates that in 57,800 adoptions by nonrelatives, 59 per cent of the placements were made by social agencies (Children's Bureau, 1962, 27).

Social work brought into being standards of child placement intended to protect the child as the weakest party. In the belief that only orderly procedures, governed by such standards, could assure to children a maximum chance of getting into good families, social work has long sought to limit child placing services to licensed agencies. This involved first of all an incessant stream of information and propaganda aimed at educating the public, potential adopters, and practictioners in other professional fields, such as medicine and law. A second step was to obtain legislation that would forbid any third party, not licensed as a child-placing agency, to charge for child-placing services. In the course of this campaign, carried out in the United States for over a quarter of a century, the official social work point of view was carried to the public by all the mass media of communication.

If a group seeks a monopoly of practice through public licensing, it must of necessity claim special competence. Social work in child placement did so, and it concentrated especially on its purported facilities for infant testing and for matching child with adoptive couple. A collection of social work pamphlets, current in the early 1950's, and directed toward potential adopters, provided a basis for a qualitative analysis of the field's claims of competence. A number of quotations will serve as examples of some of the themes which seemed typical of that literature.

Claims of Competence: Infant Testing Infant testing represented the attempt by the placement agency to scientifically predict and rationally deal with the potential of the young child available for adoption. Claims for the effectiveness of such procedures were of the following order:

> Between the foster mother, the agency's nurse, social worker, doctor, and psychiatrist, the agency gets to know him (the child) very well. By the time a baby is three months old, it can know a great deal about him—his mind, his body, his emotions. It can gauge what kind of family he needs. When he is younger than that, it can't be so sure. That's why many agencies will not place babies under three months old (Carson, 1951, 24-26).

> Free lancing doesn't pay in adoption. Go to a good licensed adoption or child-placing agency. You don't want just any child. You want one who will fit into your family (Children's Bureau, 1947, 3-4).

> An agency . . . takes time to study the child, to make as sure as possible that adopting parents will not have some unknown grief

ahead of them, like a child's mind that never develops (Carson, 1951, 4).

You want to know something about his heritage, his physical and mental development, his emotional stability, and above all you want to know his potentialities (Oklahoma State Department of Social Welfare, no date, current in 1951).

Infant tests were believed to aid substantially in eliminating those liabilities of physical, emotional, and mental makeup which are known or assumed to be inheritable. The claims that only the licensed social agency could help the adopters to avoid getting children with hereditary defects, promised a reduction in the risk which some pepole felt was connected with adoption. Some degree of risk is, of course, always involved for couples having their own children. But somehow people ordinarily do not enter pregnancy with thoughts of deformed or mentally deficient offspring. Like auto accidents and mental illness, such untoward events always seem to occur to "other people" and we consider ourselves immune. This attitude, coupled with a usually quite unwarranted pride in the exceptional qualities of our own "stock," probably fosters the view that adoption of a child born to others is more of a risk than having a child of one's own. The social work emphasis on testing for hereditary potential of the child was therefore liable to reinforce any strongly "biologistic" or "hereditarian" sentiments which the adopters already harbored. These are cues from which the childless actors need to free themselves.

Claims of Competence: Matching

(A licensed agency) . . . places a child in your home who is as far as possible like the child who might have been born to you and who is likely to grow into the kind of person who can share your family's interests and be looked on as your child. Licensed agencies generally try to find a child whose physical characteristics, mental capacities, personality, nationality, and religious background are comparable to those of the adoptive parents (Louisiana Department of Public Welfare, 1950, 2).

> It is the concern of the agency that the right adoptive home be found for each child—that you as adoptive parents accept your child as a part of your family. The agency can do this only if it knows the child's background, his physical and mental development, his personality, and his potentialities (Oklahoma State Department of Social Welfare, no date, current in 1951).

In so far as a belief in matching induces the adopters to think of the adopted child as a near replica of the one they might have had by birth, they are hardly being helped to orient themselves toward the reality of their nonfecundity. Infant testing, and matching of intellectual and emotional characteristics for any but older children, happen to be scientifically unsound. As cues to adoptive parents, the sentiments inherent in these processes are unrealistic and misleading.

In this brief inspection of some of the sentiments which social work has indirectly emphasized for adoptive parents, no mention has been made of the many constructive and important contributions which that field has made to the well-being of adoptive families. The reader may want to bear in mind that any inappropriate cues derived from the emphasis on infant testing and matching were among the unintended and unforeseen results of claims of competence once put forward with conviction and more recently questioned by the field itself.

ATTITUDES TOWARD ADOPTION IN THE COMMUNITY AT LARGE

We shall now turn to examine the stimuli which the audience at large tends to provide our actors. What do people generally think about adopting and what values are related to this event? In 1952, a study was conducted in Eastern City (a pseudonym for a university city in upstate New York). A sample of 1 per cent of the addresses in the city directory provided a basis for 183 interviews. One adult resident in each household was interviewed. Because the data from the Eastern City study were so limited in time and geography, it was partially replicated in an eastern Canadian metropolis in 1956-1957. The sentiment patterns found in Eastern City were, by and large, shown to hold good in the Canadian metropolis.

As might be expected, Eastern City residents were overtly very much accepting of adoption. But what we need to know is how people feel below the usual veneer of polite assent. Answers to a number of questions revealed that there was indeed considerable hesitation about adoption, as in this case:

Question 42	*Answers (in per cent)*	
Some people say that it's less of a risk to adopt a child than to have one by birth and others think adopting is more of a risk. Which do you think?	Less of a risk	6
	More of a risk	56
	Same amount of risk	30
	Don't know (or qualified)	7
	No answer	1

More than half of the respondents considered adopting to involve a greater risk than biological parenthood.

The following two questions were asked in different parts of the interview:

> In your opinion, how many children should there be in an ideal size family?
>
> When a couple who can't have a child decide to adopt instead, what do you think would be the ideal number of children for their adopted family?

Nearly two-thirds of the respondents differentiated between the ideal size for biological and adoptive families, the ideal size adoptive family consistently seen smaller. While 60 per cent of the respondents thought adoptive families to be ideal with one or two children, only 18 per cent felt one or two children were ideal for biologically formed families. Two children were most often named ideal for adoptive families, while four children were considered most often ideal for biological families. Very similar results were obtained in 1956 in the replication of the Eastern City Study, conducted in the Canadian Metropolis Study.

What could prompt such judgments? It seemed reasonable to suppose that people think of the adoptive family as ideally small simply because it is widely held that fewer children are available than there are people seeking to adopt. However, this is evidently not the sole basis for the view that the adoptive family is ideally small. An Eastern City respondent volunteered the explanation that "adoption is a greater social responsibility." Analysis of the response patterns from the Eastern City survey revealed that beliefs in the desirability of a small adoptive family were statistically associated with the view of biological motherhood as superior to motherhood by adoption. This "biological definition of the maternal role" was vividly illustrated in the answers to the following questions:

Question 46	*Answers (in per cent)*	
A woman was once asked whether she preferred her son by birth to her adopted son. She said: "If they were drowning and I could save only one of them, so help me, I don't know which I would choose." Do you think this mother's feeling is natural or not so natural?	Natural	76
	Not so natural	19
	Don't know (or qualified)	4
	No answer	1

Question 47	*Answers (in per cent)*	
Suppose a mother actually were faced with having to choose between two boys. If she could do nothing else, which of them would you say she should *try* to *save first*—the son by birth or the adopted son?	Son by birth	46
	Adopted son	3
	Don't know unfair question can't answer	29
	The nearest one	17
	No answer	5

In question 46 the adoptive mother represents the champion

of egalitarian values: she refuses to admit any preferences for her son by birth. The vast majority of our respondents approve of her stand, for it is in harmony with the equality with which the cultural script requires all parents to treat their children. But when question 47 asked them to make a choice, nearly half of our respondents favored the son by birth. They expect a good mother to give her son by birth the first chance, much as she would love both boys equally. For those who hold the "blood is thicker than water" point of view, there is apparently an inherent, constitutional logic, more compelling than affection. The same sentiment is also reflected in replies to a question about the proper person to raise the child born out of wedlock:

Question 73	*Answers (in per cent)*	
Would you say that it's usually better if an unmarried mother lets her child be adopted by a married couple, or would you say it's usually better if she raises the child?	Better if child is adopted	39
	Better if she raised child	40
	Depends	14
	Don't know	5
	No answer	2

A large proportion of respondents felt that the biological relationship is preferable to that of adoption. Here the emphasis on biological forces, on fecundity, is once again demonstrated. The mother with the better, the "natural" know-how is the biological mother, in spite of the social disadvantage of the absence of full family life for the child.

However, these sentiments are not uniformly represented in the various socio-economic groupings of our sample. Thus in question 47, the higher the respondent's formal educational achievement the smaller the likelihood that he would give the discriminatory response "son by birth" and the more likely was he to say "grab the nearest one" or to plead that the question was unfair. A similar relationship was found between the respondents' educational level and answers to question 73:

Table 3
Party Considered Most Suitable to Raising the Child Born Out of Wedlock, by Respondents' Educational Level (in per cent)

Who Should Raise the Child?	*Grade School and Some High School* (N = 51)	*High School Graduate* (N = 41)	**College** (N = 53)
Own mother	73	56	27
Adoptive parents	27	44	73

Pre-eminence of sentiments favoring biological parenthood were major findings from both the Eastern City and the Canadian Metropolis Studies. While it is true that age and socio-economic position influenced the relative incidence of expression of such sentiments, our study results suggest that stimuli discriminating against adoptive parenthood were part of the typical experience of adopters.

ADOPTIVE PARENTS' EXPERIENCES WITH THE ATTITUDES OF OTHERS

Having learned about the environment of sentiments which surrounds adoptive familes, we can now ask what particular stimuli impinge on the parents. The adopters in the 1956 mail questionnaire study had obtained their first child in the five years between the beginning of 1950 and the end of 1954. Most of these parents therefore had young children and might reasonably be expected to remember some of the experiences they had had at the inception of their adoptive parental status. One of the questions asked of these parents in the mail questionnaire reads:

> Here is a list of some reactions which might at times be experienced by adoptive parents and children. For each kind of statement please check the appropriate columns to show whether something like this has been experienced in your family, and if it has happened, how frequently.
>
> *Type of Experience*
>
> a. An acquaintance remarks; "Isn't it wonderful of you to have taken this child!"

b. A woman says: "How lucky you are that you didn't have to go through all the trouble of pregnancy and birth like *I* had."
c. A friend asks: "Tell me, do you know anything about this child's background?"
d. A well-wisher says: "He *is* a darling baby, and after all you never know for sure how even your own will turn out."
e. Your child is asked by a playmate: "But who are your *real* parents?"
f. You are being introduced at a party and your host remarks: "They are those unselfish people with the adopted child."
g. A friend says: "This child looks so much like you he (she) could be your own."
h. Someone refers to your adopted child, saying: "He (she) is certainly lucky to have you for parents."
i. A neighbor remarks: "How well you care for your child, just like a real mother."
j. You overhear someone saying: "Isn't it wonderful that he can be such a good father to a little boy who isn't his own son."
k. A visitor says: "It surely takes a special gift to love someone else's child like your own."
l. The mother of your child's playmate remarks: "It's hard enough to know how to handle my Johnny when he's giving me trouble. I often wonder how you deal with the troublesome behavior of a child who's adopted."

Table 4 lists eight of the 12 statements adoptive parents had been asked to check. The figures not in parentheses indicate the percentage of adoptive parents, throughout our sample and in different parts of Canada and the United States, who reported having had such experiences occasionally or frequently.

People who make such remarks and ask such questions are indeed making sharp distinctions between adoptive and biological parenthood. To see that this is so, one needs merely to translate one of these remarks into the circumstances of biological parenthood: "Isn't it wonderful of you to have taken this child" becomes, "Isn't it wonderful to have produced this child," which is both absurd and offensive. Although there is some variation between the frequencies reported for different agencies and regions, by and large the figures are remarkably

Table 4

Types of Experiences with Others: By Regions and Placement Sources, Agency or Independent Mail Questionnaire Data 1956

TYPE OF EXPERIENCE ENCOUNTERED	TOTAL REPORTING 100%	PERCENTAGE OF OCCURRENCE, ALL REGIONS COMBINED*	PERCENTAGES OF OCCURRENCE BY REGIONS*						
			AGENCIES						INDEPENDENT ADOPTERS
			Quebec	Ontario (Protestant)	Ontario (Catholic)	New York	Ohio	California	California
Isn't it wonderful of you to have taken this child	(1522)	92	94	94	95	93	96	83	90
This child looks so much like you he (she) could be your own	(1495)	92	90	90	93	93	94	94	89
He (she) is certainly lucky to have you for parents.	(1477)	87	83	84	85	87	92	86	87
Tell me, do you know anything about this child s background?	(1513)	82	80	75	78	86	92	88	77
He *is* a darling baby, and after all, you never know for sure how even your own will turn out.	(1495)	55	57	56	67	47	56	44	58
How lucky you are that you didn't have to go through all the trouble of pregnancy and birth like *I* had.	(1479)	32	28	26	29	31	37	36	34
How well you care for your child, just like a real mother	(1483)	22	20	22	34	16	19	17	30
It surely takes a special gift to love someone else's child like your own.	(1481)	17	19	18	20	13	11	13	23

* These figures represent the percentage of the respondents reporting the event to have occurred "Occasionally" or "Frequently." The significance of differences between percentages has not been determined for this table.

uniform. For instance, "Isn't it wonderful of you . . ." is reported to have occurred occasionally or frequently by 94 per cent of the Quebec parents, by 94 per cent and 95 per cent of those in Ontario, by 93 per cent of the New Yorkers, by 96 per cent in Ohio, and by 83 per cent and 90 per cent of California Independent and Los Angeles County agency adopters respectively. By inspection of such figures it appears that adoptive parents have very much the same kind of experiences with other people, whether they live in Canada or the United States, whether East, Midwest, or West.

Table 4 thus summarizes the frequencies with which the attitudes of others were experienced by adoptive parents. The statements have been listed in descending order of the frequency with which they seemed to be part of adoptive parental experience. The response patterns were subjected to a statistical technique known as Guttman scaling (Guttman, 1944). In an attitude scale, the items fit together into a pattern which allows one to measure the strength with which the attitude is held. This requires a number of statements which are supposed to measure the attitude to be investigated. If the items formed a scale, it would indicate that they belonged to a single realm of meaning.

In our case the items did indeed prove to belong to such a scale.[2] Accordingly, we can now speak with considerable confidence of certain themes as typical of the cultural environment of adoptive parenthood. These themes are the stimuli which adoptive parents experience in contact with outsiders. We had previously seen that adopters are typically role handicapped because they have had no preparation for the possibilities of nonfecundity and adoption. Now we note that this lack of a cultural script has further consequences. People who have had no intimate contact with adoption and its meanings may unintentionally add to the burden of the adopters' role handicap by

2. See Appendix A, Notes on an Eleven-Item Guttman Scale.

remarks and questions that set the adopters and their child apart. Thus, "How good of you to have taken this child," may at first sight appear to be accepting of the act of adoption. Actually it implies that the motives which move people to become adoptive parents differ from those involved in biological parenthood. "What do you know about the child's background?" suggests that while one's own offspring is accepted as a matter of course, the family member who comes from outside must prove himself by special qualifications. In other words, such questions suggest that there are special risks attached to adoption that are not part of biological parenthood. Table 4 also demonstrates that the sentiment environment surrounding the adoptive parents has at its core a mode of thought which identifies genuine parenthood as a chain of child-bearing-and-rearing. Of necessity it throws doubt on the full competence of adoptive parents, reflected in the relatively direct statement of "How well you care for your child, just like a real mother" but also in the less direct one of "How lucky you are that you did not have to go through all the trouble of pregnancy and birth like *I* had." Such a statement seemingly praises as a positive value what is commonly known to be a loss. When it is translated into the value of work, it is revealed as an invidious point of view. Imagine someone who has a job saying to an unemployed friend or neighbor: "Lucky you, I've got to go to work while you can loaf." We are reminded that not all hardships are regarded as trouble, that indeed some hardships are necessary conditions of our happiness.

In Chapter 1, it was suggested that the psychic concomitant of role handicap is alienation. It would be helpful if we could show how the role handicap, derived from the attitudes of others, is emotionally dealt with.

Early in 1961, during the tenure of the Adoption Research Project in Southern California, Whittier College sponsored a series of public lectures which dealt with material similar to that in this book. Announcements of these lectures on "Parent-

Child Relations in Adoption" were sent to professional people and to Southern California residents who had participated in one or another of the McGill studies since 1956. A few days before the first lecture, I received a letter from a woman who had been a respondent in the 1956 mail questionnaire study. This letter illustrates both certain aspects of the role handicap and the sense of alienation which flows from it. It is here presented with the writer's permission, all identifying information having been removed.

Southern California
February 27, 1961

H. D. Kirk, Ph.D.
Whittier College
Whittier, Calif.

Dear Sir:

The other day I received the notice of your lectures on adoption. As I glanced over the topics, they brought different thoughts to mind. The March 6th and 20th lectures reminded me that adoption is a responsibility that one accepts as it brings the dilemma of "Will I love this new life that is not of my blood?" Yet I know one can.

We have a teen-age son of our own who has been denied the pleasure of brothers or sisters. Nature seemed to work against us, and I was told by the doctor to adopt a child. I've often wondered when a doctor makes this statement if he has ever tried to adopt?

Good fortune came our way, though, when our minister asked us if we were still interested in adopting. Johnny was (already in school) when "little Richard" came to us, through independent adoption, and one of my first thoughts was "Will I learn to love him?"

Richard came to us when he was a few days old, a loveable little one with the most beautiful round blue eyes, which they remained. I cared for him as I had for Johnny and nature did the rest. After his death (at less than a year), I often thought, one doesn't love their husband or wife upon first meeting but one grows in love as each shares. To me the same is true of an adopted child, for if it had been Johnny that was taken, the pain could not have been any more severe.

But my interest in adoptions is not so much the parents as the attitude of people outside the family. Yes, one hears the statement by others, "I think it's wonderful to adopt," etc. Yet, do they really mean it? Sometimes I think they lack interest, understanding, or just plain don't care.

The cruelest thing ever said to me was when Richard died. The mortician knew we had legally adopted him. Yet he called one day to fill out Richard's death certificate; this is the statement he made: "For parents shall I put, 'unknown'?"

To me he had not accepted Richard as one of us. Whether it was lack of heart, interest, or what, I don't know. Yet he was considered an educated man.

Many times in front of Johnny I was asked, "Well, what does he think of an adopted brother?" To Johnny, there wasn't a happier boy—he had a brother like the other kids.

When people would introduce me to others they would say, "This is Mrs. Wright and her new adopted baby." After a while I began to resent this, whether it was my own personal reaction, or fear, I don't know. But I felt they were not letting this child be my own. They were not accepting him. If Johnny would have been the baby, they would not have said, "This is Mrs. Wright and her new natural baby." Why keep using the word, adoption?

I spoke with the minister about this attitude of others and he made the remark, "Guess some feel one should have their own." That is wonderful if one can, but after several miscarriages, a stillborn child and ruined health, there is no other way.

Sometimes you've heard the statement "That's an adopted child for you," when one misbehaves. Yet, as John grew older and became sassier, ornery and independent, I used to think Richard surely couldn't have been any worse than this. Why do people think an adopted child isn't as natural and normal as any other child, and shouldn't misbehave?

I guess you're wondering why the letter, but as I read over the lecture topics I felt I had to share of my thoughts on adoption that have bothered me, especially outsiders' attitudes.

Thank you for taking your time to read my thoughts.

Yours truly,
(Mrs.) Elizabeth Wright (pseud.)

How are adopters to deal with such handicapping relationships and with the feelings of alienation which arise from them?

Adoptive parents may say to themselves: "I mustn't let this sort of thing bother me," and they may do well to form such attitudes; but that is different from not recognizing that the attitudes exist. In 1956, when questionnaires were sent to several thousand adoptive parents in Canada and the United States, a Los Angeles couple sent theirs back with this note attached: "You will probably be amused to know that when I first scanned your questionnaire I found these questions (referring to the attitudes of others) anachronistic. Adoptions, I said to myself, are accepted in our community. Those questions are not in good taste or ever asked. Yet when my wife and I carefully reviewed them I was surprised that we had been asked at least five of them." Note here the word "surprised." Does it not suggest that the experience had somehow been put out of the way? Surely this is quite a different action from saying to oneself: "I won't let this bother me." In subsequent chapters, we shall take a closer look at the factors that may have made this adoptive father surprised at experiences which he subsequently recognized to have happened to himself and to members of his immediate family circle.

CHAPTER THREE

*

Dilemmas of Adoptive Parenthood

*

THE reader may wonder why so much time is being devoted to what may seem minor difficulties on the way to the satisfactions and opportunities of adoptive family life. Let us therefore recall what we have started to do: We are inspecting the social and psychic foundations on which adoption rests. Only in that way can we come to understand the special nature of the adoptive relationship, both its inherent difficulties and its potential rewards. Thus, we saw that the situational discrepancies, involved in involuntary childlessness, bring about a number of role handicaps for the couple entering adoption. These handicaps make themselves felt in the realm of role preparation, role autonomy, obligations, and rewards and sanctions for role performance.

While the adoptive parent actors are fitting their outlook to the changed situation, they are encountering cues from other actors and from the audience, which tend to make this task more difficult. They must focus their attention on their capacities for rearing the child they have taken as their own. The emphasis on fecundity revealed in other people's sentiments may make them less confident of their ability and influence them to regard their parenthood as less valuable than that of fecund couples. The adopters will quite understandably try to resist such a devaluation of their role. It is therefore no surprise that our Los Angeles respondent had repressed the memory of other people's remarks that he considered not in good taste.

In order that adoptive parents can get on with their new life with maximum effectiveness, they must be able to respect the dignity of their role while they understand and accept its reality. This consideration is reflected in an important prescription for adoptive family life: that the parents should reveal to the child the fact that he was adopted. In this chapter we shall inquire into the meaning and some of the consequences of this prescription.

REVELATION: ITS MEANING TO THE PARENTS

The directive to adoptive parents to inform their children of the fact of adoption, and that they should do so early in the child's life, has been part of the professional practice in child placement for at least two decades. The prescription stems from the view that secrecy is practically impossible to achieve, however some parents might desire it, and that discovery of the fact of adoption is likely to be disturbing to the child if initiated by outsiders. Parental revelation has therefore been considered a preventive mental health step, consonant with other important cultural values, such as that of honesty between parents and children.

However, carrying the prescription out is no simple task for adoptive parents. Several of the McGill studies have drawn attention to feelings of uncertainty: when to start the telling, how much information to give, whether to initiate discussion or to wait for the child to raise questions. Most of the parents who talked about it regarded the prescription as necessary and justified, but many implied that it was not easily dealt with.

An agency financed and administered by a group of adoptive parents sent a questionnaire to its own client-members a few years ago. The questionnaire was constructed by a committee of the membership so that it may be regarded as reflecting the concerns and major ideas of that group of adoptive parents. Even on the surface, the "telling" prescription looms large in the questionnaire, which consisted of 46 questions. Twenty of these, or 43 per cent, were concerned with the subject of revelation. A close reading of these questions reveals that those who wrote them felt that the prescription poses difficulties and problems. But these difficulties only represent part of the meaning the prescription has for adoptive parents. While the difficulties it poses are recognized, the parents are also committed to carrying the prescription out. This commitment was evident from spontaneous remarks adoptive parents wrote into the 1956 mail questionnaire, from observations made among members of adoptive parent groups in California, and from the questionnaire sent to its members by the Barker Foundation in Washington, D.C. All of the 116 couples who returned their questionnaires answered the following question in the negative: "Do you think it might be better if children were not told about being adopted?" This is evidence on the intellectual side of commitment. But commitment to a point of view or to an activty also has anchors in the emotions. The emotional aspect of adoptive parental commitment to the "telling" prescription was illustrated in letters received by the editors of a leading woman's magazine in the latter part of 1959. In September of that year, the magazine published an article entitled "To My Adopted Daughter—I Wish I Had Not Told You." The issue appeared during the beginning of the study of adoptive parent groups in California. Since it called into question the wisdom of the "telling" prescription, the article seemed tailor-made for learning about the meaning which the prescription has to adoptive parents. Upon request, the editor made available for analysis the letters which the magazine had received in response to the article. A systematic inspection of these letters provided confirmation that adoptive parents, at least those like the correspondents, have considerable emotional commitment to the prescription.

Among the 184 correspondents whose letters were read, 86 were adoptive parents, 43 were adoptees, and 15 were professionals. There were also 23 letters from other readers with no special role relative to adoption and 17 letters from people whose identity was unclear. Thus, nearly half of the correspondents were adopters while fewer than one-quarter were adopted persons and only 8 per cent of the letters came from professionals. The article's main theme is summed up in these words by the author: "The knowledge that one is adopted creates far more problems than the one it is to solve." The overwhelming majority of the readers disagreed with this theme. Their disagreement ranged from 87 per cent among the adoptees, through 92 per cent among the adoptive parents, to 100 per cent among the professionals.

The letters also gave some clues concerning the intensity with which correspondents expressed their disagreement with the author's theme. The following heavily emotion-laden terms illustrate what we classified as "disagreement with strong feeling," namely: "bitter indignation," a sense of having been "infuriated," "disgusted," and "greatly disturbed."

Not all the letters could be so classified. Among the 77 classifiable letters from adoptive parents, 87 per cent expressed strong feelings in their statements of disagreement with the theme. Among 14 letters from professionals, 60 per cent disagreed in this manner, while in 34 letters from adoptees only 42 per cent did so. Adoptive parents were evidently by far the angriest and most troubled in the way in which they protested the theme of this article. All the facts we have been able to gather from this analysis point to the same conclusion: These adoptive parents were thoroughly committed to the prescription that the child should be told about his adoption.

But why should they have so great a stake in an issue which presents them with problems and difficulties? Whence arises this commitment to at least the form of the prescription? Some of the likely sources of it may be listed as follows:

1. In the preceding chapter we saw that agencies have tended to claim a special competence in child placement on the basis of infant testing and matching. Further reasons advanced on behalf of the services of adoption agencies concern the confidentiality of the procedure and the near certainty that the child cannot be successfully reclaimed by the natural parents. Under such conditions of believed and real benefits from agency services, the adopters are likely to feel committed to the point of view espoused by the professional workers. These represent authoritative knowledge and skill in areas in which the adoptive applicant feels especially ignorant and powerless to help himself.

2. White couples who seek to adopt through a licensed agency are in a "seller's market."[1] That is to say, with a low supply of white children[2] and a high demand by potential parents, the agencies can be selective in trying to find the couple they consider best suited for a particular child. This circumstance of having power over applicants permits the agency to press its advantage for compliance with the professional outlook, here embodied in the prescription that the clients must tell the child of his adoption. A report on agency practices (Shapiro, 1956: I, 87) shows that such pressure is regularly applied: ". . . most agencies specifically direct adoptive parents to inform the child early before he learns about adoption from others. 'Awareness of need to inform a must' and 'we do not accept if couple refuses' were comments frequently made."

1. Social work sources claim that this ratio of supply to demand is now (1962) changed in favor of potential adopters. In some areas, and for certain groups in the population, especially Jewish couples and those without religious affiliation, that change seems not to have occurred.

2. Children of non-white, especially Negro, ancestry are in high supply.

3. Once the adoptive parents have initiated "telling," they cannot very well undo the act. Having an irreversible action on their hands, their recourse will most likely be to a stout defense and justification of it.

4. This is so especially for those adoptive parents who have received one child and now seek another from the same agency. The dependency on the agency for continuing service therefore makes these clients particularly amenable to following its prescription.

5. Agency approval and the subsequent placement of a child imply positive sanctions and rewards, which tend to obligate the client to the professional benefactor.

Although at times adopters may resent the professional viewpoint, the above reasons show why they can be expected to form strong allegiance to it. A parental note, written into the 1956 mail questionnaire, illustrates this attachment to the standards of social work, but not without a query as to the procedure, which the prescription has not defined. "We were told that we must inform the baby of his adoption as soon as he understands. We feel this is good and will prevent any hurt or misunderstanding later, also the child will feel a greater trust in us for being frank with him. *P.S. (we would like to know) how people would deal with the above situation!*" [Emphasis added.]

REVELATION: SOME OF ITS CONSEQUENCES

Having assured ourselves of the fact that adoptive parents are generally committed to the prescription, we must inquire why it should present them with more or less serious difficulties. This exploration is to be cast in the context of dilemmas that face the adoptive parents in the course of their family life. We shall think of dilemmas as choices to be made between alternative goals, each demanding a contrasting price. This conception of "dilemmas" implies that it is difficult to have both goal *A* and goal *B*, and if one of them is clearly chosen, a price has to be paid in the loss of the goal thereby excluded. Kirkpatrick (1955, 85-92) has developed a list of common family dilemmas which confront people in American life, especially in the middle class. One of these is stated here to illustrate the type of thing we will do more specifically with respect to adoption. North American parents face, among other dilemmas, the dilemma between *A,* the goal of flexible, general training, and *B,* rigid, specific training for their children. If goal *A* (flexible general training) is chosen, the child is likely to be more inventive and socially adaptable—perhaps a useful solution in a world in which "anything could happen." But we note also that, if this avenue to child training is chosen, there is the distinct possibility that the child will become a dilettante, for to be prepared for everything is to be prepared for nothing in particular. Thus, in a world in which occupational tasks are increasingly specialized such a child may have considerable difficulty in finding, and fitting into, a proper occupational place in terms of technical competence. If goal *B,* (*i.e.,* rigid and specific training) is chosen, a price of failure may have to be paid when under changed circumstances a different knowledge and another set of skills are required. This is a dilemma which is especially pertinent to parental responsiblities as they intersect with the responsibilities of the school.

1. *The Dilemma of Enchantment vs. Disenchantment in Parental Role Definition* The terms "enchantment" and "disenchantment" used here carry quite specific meanings. To define them let us once again take refuge in the language of the drama, in the situation of the actor and the play, the stage and the audience. Let us first think of certain types of dramas as we know them in the folk epics, in the great legends, and in the fairy tales. There the audience knows the outcome from the start, for the drama is cast in a setting of a philosophy of wholeness. The universe portrayed in these dramas is fixed, closed, and final. In the plot, the actors and the audience alike know the difference between right and wrong clearly, as be-

tween good and evil, and they also know that certain forces will finally triumph over others because it is preordained. In an enchanted plot, the actors play parts of a plan which presupposes wholeness and which enshrines flawlessness. If misfortune befalls the actor who represents the good, he is miraculously saved; or through his suffering he may fulfil a special mission which has redemptive consequences for the community. He may be carried safely in the stomach of a whale, or remain unhurt by wild animals or raging fire. If in the course of struggles, which are part of the drama between good and evil, the actor loses a limb or even his head, it may be returned to him and he restored to his orignal state of wholeness. Thus the world view, the plot, and the role are indicative of the meaning of enchantment as we employ it here; they each indicate an undivided whole, a seamless robe, reflecting the "original" and the "natural" order of things.

The disenchanted world view, drama, and role, carry no such implications of wholeness or completeness, nor of preordained certainty as to the way the plot will end. Here man is more or less on his own. What saves him is his superior ability, his greater capacity to understand and to adapt to his environment, whether through feeling, or intellect, or both. If in this situation of disenchantment the actor is hurt in the struggle, if he is maimed, he must rely on his ingenuity, or that of his fellows, in his desire to adapt himself. Here the old situation is never magically restored. The previous wholeness is gone forever, if indeed it was there before, and the partial, the artificial, the substitutive takes its place. Instead of a seamless robe, the disenchanted situation posits at most a garment of standard cut and seams which, after having been torn and mended, becomes a patched robe. In our society, parenthood is still widely held enchanted—that is, whole and indivisible—from the beginning of the love of mates, through conception, pregnancy, birth, and child rearing. It is thus regarded by many of our contemporaries as a part of a drama in which sentiment and tradition predominate over rationality and personal choice. This may explain why in Eastern City at least half of our respondents considered it best for the child born out of wedlock to be raised by the natural mother and why adoption, which is commonly regarded proper only as a last resort, was not viewed as making for a parenthood as sturdy as that of the "natural," the "original" type.

What then is the dilemma of role definitions to which we have referred by the terms "Enchantment" *vs.* "Disenchantment"? The dilemma for adoptive parents consists essentially in what picture of themselves and their role they select for themselves. They can either say to themselves, "I am just like any other parent," and reject the objective and subjective differences we identified earlier. If they choose this way of defining themselves and their place in the drama, they will be rewarded by conforming to the regulation model of parenthood and thus feeling fewer pangs about the differences visible to the audience beyond the stage. But such adoptive parents will more likely pay a price in the process of seeking and keeping sound relations with their principal fellow-actors, namely their children, around the meaning of adoption. If, on the other hand, they choose to acknowledge their differences by retaining a memory of their original deprivations and a recognition of their current substitute position on the stage, then their problem will more likely be with the audience rather than with their fellow-actors.

2. *The Dilemma of Integration vs. Differentiation* In the family drama the new-born who joins the procreative pair is as yet something of a stranger. We are reminded of this when we hear of mothers who confide that at first sight they do not feel the warmth and maternal closeness toward the child which are part of the folklore-notion of the role. We know further that this sense of common membership grows in the course of the relationship with the infant. Indeed, it grows principally because of the parental service rendered to the child in his utter helplessness.

While we may agree that in the biological family the child

must still be made into a member, we also recognize that he is already so identified at arrival with no qualifications. Now, however, we focus on the activities of the kin group, which through a variety of acts aids the couple in integrating the new member, in making themselves feel the reality of his membership, and thus drawing him closer to them. We saw already that many of the circumstances that come to the assistance of natural parents in this process of integrating the new child are absent in the case of adopters. We must therefore assume that the latter will work harder at this labor of love in which the stranger is turned into a member. This assumption is borne out by the statements of teachers and other observers of the parent-child relationship who claim that adoptive parents tend more readily toward overprotection of their children than biological parents.

The goal of integration then is the common goal of all parents. This goal is closely linked to a second one that posits that children shall be allowed progressive freedoms, that once truly part of the family they shall increasingly be given opportunities for independence. This is the goal of differentation in which the child is to be weaned, first from the breast or bottle, then the hand, and finally the mind of his parents. And, as the child moves out into the play group, the school, and beyond, into his own loves and attachments, he becomes a person in his own right. For this process of over-all weaning, it is apparently nceessary for the child first to have had the firmest and warmest of attachments, a deeply anchored love and feeling of group membership. When this process has successfully culminated in the creation of a new identity we say: "He knows who he is"; whereby we mean two other things: "We know who he is" and "He knows where he stands, among whom he belongs." We may now state the normal parental goal in our society as one that involves progressive differentiation of their children on a firmly established base of integration.

The adoptive parents' dilemma, however, is that they are expected to engage in differentiating acts practically from the start of the relationship with the child. The parents are counseled to use the word "adopted" in conjunction with gestures of endearment. But children do not remain inarticulate; before long they will want to ask about the word and the circumstances surrounding it. The implication of the prescription, as reflected in this dilemma, is that the adoptive parents must begin to differentiate the child out of their midst, declare him to be different at the very time when they also feel especially strongly the desire to attach him to themselves and themselves to him. It will be recalled that they are, during several months, still not officially the child's parents and therefore struggle especially hard to maintain the line of hoped-for parenthood, through their faith in what they hope will be. Their dilemma, therefore, is whether they shall, at least for a time, abstain from speaking of adoption or whether they shall use the word as the mental health professions have suggested it. In a long term sense, the dilemma is, of course, that of concealment of the fact of adoption as against its revelation. If they should temporarily or more permanently seek to conceal it (and it is done successfully by some) the adoptive parents will pay the price of those feelings of guilt which are the lot of those who offend against certain valued beliefs which they themselves ordinarily hold. But the parents gain thereby the satisfaction that their child need not worry about his past, his forebears; and the adoptive parents are spared the burden of feeling their way along an uncertain road in child rearing, a burden which comes with the revelation, as the child is older. The penalty of choosing the goal of candidness, then, consists in uncertainty as to their proper and appropriate parental acts on the basis of the unknown relationship that results from the candidness. This uncertainty is reflected in the following questions and remarks volunteered in the pages of the 1956 mail questionnaire:

> What effect on the child has the knowledge that he or she is adopted?

(We need to know about) the reactions of the child on hearing he's adopted—Ours already know but are still young and so the full awareness is not there yet. Prospective adopting parents may feel concern over this one bridge to be crossed.

In future questionnaires we would be interested in learning some of the methods used (by others) in explaining adoption to young children.

3. *The Dilemma of Ignorance vs. Knowledge of the Child's Background* In the history of adoption work there was a time when social agencies thought it necessary to share with adoptive applicants everything the social work staff knew about an available child's background. Adoptive parents are said to have wanted every possible assurance that the child's background was "untainted" and frequently pressed for information. But there seem to have been subtle changes in the meaning of adoption; it appears that adopters are now markedly more ready to accept risks than they were two or three decades ago. This change is reflected in the clamor by adopting couples for infants as young as possible after birth. On the side of the professionals this change was stimulated by Bowlby's classic World Health monograph (Bowlby, 1951), which summarized the results of several studies on maternal deprivation. Many agencies have apparently also modified their policies as to the amount of information to be given. In the 1954 Study of Agency Practice conducted by the Child Welfare League (Schapiro, 1956: I, 86), half of 257 agencies reported that they did not give complete background information. In the other half, who said they gave complete information, some apparently qualified this by saying they gave "selected background material." The consensus of delegates to the 1955 Child Welfare Conference on Adoption was: "It is unsound practice to give information about a condition around which there is common prejudice, and which, from a scientific standpoint, cannot adversely affect the child's development and full acceptance by the family" (Schapiro, 1956: I, 87).

The dilemma for the adoptive parents consists of what they shall do with the information which the agency provides them. Shall they (a) take that information seriously and record it? Or shall they (b) try to forget about it? If they choose (a), they may be able to answer more intelligently and specifically a physician's questions about the child's health background when the child is ill, but they will also have more specific occasions to think of the child as different from themselves. If they choose (b), and forget what the agency told them, they may be able to identify themselves more fully with the child, but they will then lack pertinent information needed for or by the child at times of crisis, such as illness or the child's move into adulthood. Some parents seem to feel that, if they know nothing about the child's background, they can then say truthfully that they do not, when the child inquires. But what this parental ignorance does to the child and to the parent-child relationship is not known. A couple who had just legally adopted their first child received a copy of the court order in the mail. In a panic the adoptive father called up the agency and inquired whether he might destroy the document. He and his wife did not want to be reminded of the child's original name. In a way then, this dilemma poses the problem whether or not the adoptive parents shall choose to think about the child's origins.

4. *The Dilemma of Reproductive Morals vs. the Principle of Respect for Individual Personality* Finally there is the dilemma of how adoptive parents are to feel and think about the child's original parents. For many, though not all, adoptive parents this dilemma refers to the circumstances of the child's birth. It is the dilemma of whether to admit to the child that he was born out of wedlock, and if to admit it, how to do so without either slandering his forebears or letting down the obligation that the norms of sexual behavior are to be taught to children in the context of premarital chastity. Because of their conflict between the desire to bring their children up along lines of

"proper" sanctioned sexual conduct and the desire to spare the reputation of the child's natural parents, this has been called the dilemma of reproductive morals vs. the principle of respect for individual personality. In a subsequent chapter a great deal more will be said about this particular dilemma and the way it may be minimized. At this point little more can be done than to point to its existence and to indicate that this is the area in which adoptive parents exhibit the least self-confidence, the issue from which they seem to shy away most. This is indeed serious for them, since it is common knowledge that the largest number of children adopted by nonrelatives are born out of wedlock. What is common knowledge becomes also our children's knowledge. This is why adoptive parents are forced to make their choice between the alternatives the dilemma offers. And whichever side they choose will, they fear, bring damage to the child and to their family unity.

In summary, we have in this chapter considered the prescription of relevation, shown that parents are committed to it, and have indicated several reasons for this commitment. Finally we suggested four dilemmas which arise out of the compliance with the prescription.

It may have become obvious that the dilemmas which derive from the prescription constitute a further development of the role handicap of adoptive family life. This role handicap is not one of "minor difficulties." It covers the whole family cycle; and it relates to their view of themselves as parents, their relationship with the child, and their attitude toward the child's forebears.

In the following chapter we shall consider how adoptive parents try to deal with their role handicap.

CHAPTER FOUR

*

Coping with Role Handicap

*

IN previous chapters we identified handicapping circumstances usually preceding or accompanying adoption, as well as certain dilemmas which tend to carry the handicap over into later phases of adoptive family life. Now we shall ask how adoptive parents try to cope with the handicap and the consequent alienation.

Let us briefly recall the dilemmas as they had been described: First, there is the question of how adoptive parents are to see themselves. Are they to regard themselves as just ordinary parents, no different from biological parents (which is the choice of "enchantment")? Or are they to regard themselves as different, indeed as substitute parents (the choice of "disenchantment")? Second, there is the dilemma of how the parents are to relate themselves to the child. Are they to emphasize his difference while they are trying to become a family (the choice of differentiation simultaneous with integration) or are they to go ahead with integrative acts without the conflicting demands of relevation? The third dilemma poses the question whether the adoptive parents are to record and try to recall background information about the child. This, in a sense, is a choice between knowledge and ignorance of the child's forebears. The fourth dilemma primarily concerns the adoptive parents whose children were born out of wedlock. Their dilemma consists of how to teach two moral imperatives, each with its claim on the parents: Are they to indoctrinate the child with the necessity for premarital chastity (the choice of reproductive moral standards)? Or are they to make less of these norms than ordinarily required, so as to protect the good reputation of the child's natural parents who bore him out of wedlock (the choice of the ethic of respect for the individual)?

It is in the nature of dilemmas that they cannot be fully solved. Something must be sacrificed in the course of choosing. We cannot ever have our cake and eat it too. The task in this chapter will be to explore the ways along which adoptive parents currently seek to cope with these common dilemmas. This implies that we are going to inquire into the means which adoptive parents use in their attempts at adapting to the conditions of their role handicap.

THE PLACE OF THEORY

Before we begin to explore in detail these aspects of parental behavior, indeed to make such an exploration understandable, it is first necessary to broach a related subject. We must raise the question of theory. In North America there has long been a curious folklore about theoretical thinking, as if it were the opposite of practical endeavors. But it has also been observed that nothing is so practical as a good theory. Theory serves as a map. On this map we can identify and order what we already know. We can sketch in what we believe, but are not certain, to exist. Such a "map" was made by the Russian chemist Mendeleev in the nineteenth century. He drew up the Periodic

Table, which systematically ordered the property of elements. Mendeleev's Table made possible the prediction of certain new elements which were only theoretically, and not practically, "known" by him. But because of his "map," his theoretical layout of the properties of elements, the course of practical discovery was greatly advanced.

There are two very practical aspects to theory: Theory organizes what we know; it makes sense of this knowledge by connecting different parts of it. A good map tells us the spatial relations between river and town and highway. Once we have such a map we travel in that area with more confidence. Theory is practical in another sense also. The areas that have not yet been thoroughly explored may be sketched in on the map. Such an area on the map exerts a pull toward discovery. It poses the problem of what *might* exist there. It is the area of speculation, of educated guesses, of hypotheses. So theory, as a kind of mapping of reality, allows men to ask more sensible questions about it. Of course, frequently the explorers find that the reality differs considerably from what they had presumed it to be. Then, with their added knowledge, they must remake their map to fit it to the reality of which they are now aware. In very rough outlines, this is what theory does for men in a practical way.

This book seeks to present a theory of adoptive relations. Knowledge gained from a number of studies has been fitted together into a pattern whereby relevant structures can be identified and their operation observed. If that work has been done properly it should provide a more reliable map of certain aspects of adoptive relations than was available heretofore.

Theory and research go hand in hand. There are times when one flounders and seems to be learning nothing. Later one may discover that what was sought was very close by, but it remained "invisible" because one did not look in the right place or even know exactly what to look for. Often this was so in the adoption studies. But there were also important highlights of discovery.

Like flares in the night, they suddenly illuminated the territory through which only poor headway had been made. To let the reader understand the theory being developed, it will be desirable to provide certain information about the course of the inquiry.

Signposts to the Proposed Theory Among the events which served as signposts to a theory of adoptive relations were two which seem especially suitable to illustrate its development. Both of these events involve the mail questionnaire study of 1956. Sometime in 1955, plans were being made for exploration of the attitudes and experiences of adoptive parents. At such a time of preliminary planning, one gathers all possible clues to the dimensions and meanings of the area to be studied. One wants to make the most educated guesses possible about the object of the proposed research. That is why results from a small pilot study of 1952 were re-examined. In that pilot investigation 97 adoptive couples had filled out a rather elementary questionnaire. One question was meant to inquire into the atitudes which other people direct toward adoptive parents. It was phrased in this way: "Has anyone ever made an unfriendly remark, or done something unpleasant or troublesome for you or your child, because they knew that the child is adopted?" Most of the respondents said no, some said that they could not remember, and only 15 out of 97 reported that something unpleasant had occurred. Furthermore, of these few affirmative replies, only 8 told anything specific of what had happened. Thus, this approach had not been effective as a means of exploring the attitudes of others. If one wanted to look more critically at this area, it was necessary to furnish better tools for the investigation.

In 1955, a new questionnaire was drafted. Its utility was to be tested with the help of groups of adoptive couples. Through the good offices of the director of the Children's Service Centre of Montreal, two groups of couples were called together. The first one met for an evening on the agency's premises. The group consisted of 11 couples who were seated together in the boardroom. At the start of the meeting they had been briefed about the purpose of the gathering as a test of the questionnaire. They were instructed to answer as they would normally do if the questionnaire came to their home, but to be especially critical of the meanings of questions. Approximately in the middle of the questionnaire there was the old question which had failed in 1952 to give any useful results. As host, I was free to move about the room and could observe what happened when a couple came to that question. There were various reactions to it. One couple seemed to stiffen, the man shrugging his shoulder while his wife turned the page to the next question without giving an answer. Another couple looked at each other with a puzzled expression and likewise turned the page without answering. A third couple whispered with seeming agitation, and proceeded to the next question. Later, when the questionnaires were checked, it was noticed that 10 out of 11 couples had left the question unanswered. Only one had answered it and they had done it by writing a large NO over the entire page, as if to blot out the question itself. It was clear that this question was anxiety provoking. At the time, I interpreted this anxiety as stemming from the attitudes of others with which the question had dealt. This interpretation must now be regarded as oversimplified.

When it became evident that these couples refused to deal with the question, it seemed that once again we would be met with failure, that adoptive parents' experiences with the attitudes of other people could not be seen by this route. Clearly something drastically different was called for. At this point it is necessary to tell the ensuing events of the meeting as personal history. As researcher, I felt frustrated at the continued failure. Looking back at what happened in that situation I am again astonished at the way the problem was solved.

To understand what occurred, it is necessary to have a picture of the meeting place. The boardroom in which the meeting was held adjoined the director's office, the two being separated by an accordion door which ran the whole width of the room. On that evening the two rooms had been made into one. The visting couples were seated in a semicircle in the boardroom. Farther over, in the director's office, my wife was arranging a table of refreshments.

The incident to be related occurred during the discussion of the questions. When half of the questionnaire had been dealt with and the question about the attitudes of other people had been reached, I said, "Well, what about this one?" While there had been considerable discussion just a few moments before, things were suddenly very quiet in the room. I suppose that people were tense. I certainly was. Meanwhile I had decided on a plan of action, though I was not prepared for the events it initiated. I left the semicircle of couples and walked to the middle of the adjoining office. Then I addressed my wife who at that moment had her back to the group and was cutting a cake. "Ruth," I said quietly, "do you remember the night when we were outside the Children's Ward of X County Hospital, after Francie who was then two years old, had had her tonsils out? We were drowsing in chairs outside the ward, having taken shifts earlier in the day because of the inadequate nursing service there. And do you remember how, about two or three o'clock in the morning, our acquaintance, Mary L., came by? She had been visiting her husband who was critically ill. As she passed us she said: 'Well, if it isn't the Kirks; what are you doing here at this hour?' You remember that you told Mrs. L. about Francie's tonsillectomy, and that she remarked, 'Why that's just like a real mother!' "

I waited a few seconds, then I added: "Ruth, how did it make you feel?" There was quite a long pause and I must admit I was getting to feel a bit guilty at having put my wife into such a predicament among these strangers. When she finally spoke it was with a voice I could hardly recognize as hers. It was choked—she was obviously trying to hold back her tears.

Still standing with her back to the group and to me, she said just one word: "Awful."

At this point I turned to the group and saw all the people looking very solemn, if not sullen. It seemed as if a wall of impenetrable faces had been put up to keep me out of forbidden territory. My original plan had been to return to my place by the table and to take up the question of other pepole's attitudes. However, I must have been caught up in the tensions which the incident had caused. Instead of carrying on as I had intended, I walked over to the first couple on my right and said to the woman: "You heard how Mrs. Kirk felt, how did *you* feel?" The lady mumbled: "Awful, too," wiped her eyes, and left the room. Her husband followed her. I felt as if things were rapidly collapsing. No one said anything, until a few minutes later when the first couple returned to the room. The wife now smiled a little and said quietly, "Sorry to have made this commotion; it just hit me hard because what happened to me had been so much like what happened to you." Then she told us her story. Presently most of the other couples were contributing theirs. What only a few moments earlier had looked like a major calamity had turned into one of the most productive research sessions of my experience.

The reader has probably guessed by now that the question about other people's attitudes, which was later put into the mail questionnaire, was constructed from the reports these couples had provided. And that they had told about real events which were genuine and typical also for adopting parents across this continent became evident when the answers to the mail questionnaires were returned. Now over 90 per cent of the parents admitted to specific items of experience with other people, while a few years before fewer than 10 per cent had given such information. The discussion of that evening in 1955 had been productive for research. But only much later was it discerned that it was also a signpost to a theory of adoptive relations.

The sense in which this was so will become evident presently.

A second signpost to this theory was provided by an event which occurred nearly two years later, in 1957. By then over 1,500 of the questionnaires from 1956 had been returned and a statistical study of most of the questions had been completed. One part of the questionnaire had defied attempts at systematic analysis. The page which followed the twelve items identifying the attitudes of others had opened this way: "Please add here any other experiences regarding the adoption which were especially important to you." Halfway down the page, which was otherwise left blank, the respondents were asked: "Are there any important matters relating to adoption which you would have liked seen included in this questionnaire?" This page was actually meant to give the respondents a chance to blow off steam, to enable them to get off their chests some of the tensions, built up by preceding questions. There was reason to believe that this type of ventilation would be in the interest of getting respondents to complete their questionnaire, once they had started. When the forms were returned, it was evident that the idea had worked. Many of these pages had been crammed full and many others had writing added on the back. When the material was read, much of it proved fascinating, but it was not clear what use could be made of it, what light it could shed on adoptive relations. The subject matter mentioned on that page ranged very wide, so that a listing of it hardly seemed helpful. The recurring and intriguing question was whether any major messages or themes could be detected in these relatively spontaneous writings. Eventually two such themes were indeed shown to pervade that material. Before they are named, these themes bear identification through examples:

Theme 1: Having George has been a privilege. . . .
We feel honored to be adopted parents.
We feel especially blessed with both children. *We still feel like pinching ourselves.* (Emphasis added.)

Feel we're lucky to have children.

Our feeling is that we are the fortunate ones by getting the children.

You should ask people if they realize how lucky they are to get such a precious gift.

Theme 2: We are telling our daughter she is adopted but it is hard for us to realize this ourselves. We feel almost as though we were telling her an untruth.

We do not feel he is adopted.

It has never entered our minds that she has ever belonged to anyone else but us.

In New Jersey, after the legal formalities are arranged, we are no longer adopting parents but are legally certified as natural parents and the matter of adoption need never arise.

Interpretation To be "privileged," "lucky," or unbelieving of one's good luck to the point of "pinching" oneself suggests that one is different from those around him who are inclined to take the enjoyment of a particular experience as a right, for granted. Statements in Theme 1 were therefore regarded as acknowledging some difference between the situation of natural and adoptive parenthood. The theme was called "Acknowledgment-of-Difference."

Theme 2 suggests a kind of withdrawal from, perhaps a denial, of what is known to be true. It is called "Rejection-of-Difference." Here was an indication that adoptive parents who emphasized Theme 2 had the wrong cues for carrying out their new roles. But as this idea was pursued further, it was found that both themes frequently were present in a single respondent's reply. It became clear that the research would have to focus on the ways in which adoptive parents regarded themselves, what picture they had of themselves and of their roles.

Once the idea of these two themes as conflicting orientations toward the adoptive situation had suggested itself, a number of other matters became more understandable. It explained why the Los Angeles respondent had been "surprised" at finding that matters he regarded as outdated actually had occurred to members of his own family. It also explained why people in the group meeting at first balked at dealing with the questions about other people's attitudes. The reasoning followed these lines: Early experiences preceding adoption are difficult and, as the parents move into adoption, they find that their troubles are by no means over. Their situation is comparable to that of persons who have had an operation to remove the cause of a painful condition. When the pain persists long after the operation, the patient may be inclined to crave means to deal solely with the painful symptom. His use of anesthetizing drugs is certainly understandable. It is normal enough for people to seek ways of making their difficulties bearable.

Such considerations led to the formulation of the themes of "Rejection-of-Difference" and "Acknowledgment-of-Difference" as representative of the two ways of coping with the role handicap of adoptive parenthood. It was a vital step in the development of the theory and led to a reanalysis of the main elements of adoptive parental behavior. Everything known about such behavior was listed and each item was submitted to the query of what the practice means in terms of coping: Did it appear to be an example of "acknowledgment" or of "rejection-of-difference" patterns? In other words, the activities of adopters were treated as if they all could serve as means of coping with role handicap. These behavior patterns are now to be identified and ordered into categories of "acknowledgment-of-difference" and "rejection-of-difference."[1] Wherever possible they will be illustrated with examples from questionnaire entries.

PATTERNS SUGGESTING "REJECTION-OF-DIFFERENCE"

It is common in North American jurisdictions to issue new birth certificates at the time of the legalization of adoptions.

1. This categorical listing is based on a single investigator's judgments and must therefore be treated as purely suggestive.

These certificates show the child's new name, making no reference to a former status. Though undoubtedly in the child's interest in the sense that he can not be shamed before others, as in school, this document also serves as an institutional sanction for "rejection-of-difference" on the parents' part: "In New Jersey, after the legal formalities are arranged, we are no longer adopting parents but are *legally certified as natural parents* and the matter of adoption need never arise." (Emphasis added.)

Most adoptive parents report having been asked about the child's background; they typically respond with irritation:

> Such a question is uncalled for.
>
> It's none of their business.
>
> Remark: "Is that your real baby?"
> Reply: "If you will be kind enough to forgive me for not answering that question, I shall be happy to forgive you for asking it."
>
> Remark: "Were her parents married?"
> Reply: "Yes, we were married almost ten years before she was born."

Such responses indicate that adopters are at a loss for a measured reply. Waiting until they are attacked, they can do little but to fend off the inquiries.

Matching of appearance, race, and nationality respectively seem to be relatively common. The closer the appearance and background of parents and child, the less likelihood that other people will observe differences. Adoptive parents who answered the 1956 mail questionnaire showed themselves fairly detached from matching by appearance, 48 per cent of the husbands and 50 per cent of the wives saying that they thought it quite unimportant. Even greater detachment existed in the area of the child's nationality background. Only in the matter of race was the large majority of adopters in favor of a homogeneous family. Three-quarters of all the respondents said that matching by race was very important.

The adoptive family can be made to look similar to the biological family by three other devices. Aside from the personal satisfactions usually derived from caring for a child during his early infancy, having an infant also helps the adoptive parents to "pass" for biological parents: "Our preference was for a very young infant in the early weeks of life. The younger the child the more nearly the adopted situation parallels the normal having of children." By adopting at intervals of not less than nine months or a year, adopters can simulate the spacing in the arrival of children by birth. Also, in biological families the order of children determines their ages relative to each other. Although, theoretically, adoptive parents could take a second or third child who is older than the ones who precede him, this is hardly ever done. The simulation of the biological family along these various lines is thus a form of adaptation to role handicap through "rejection-of-difference."

The adoptive parent who strives toward integrating his child into the family but who follows the prescription to reveal the fact of adoption to him, may seek to minimize the impact of this revelation by assurance of his love: "I probably wouldn't tell them if I knew they'd never find out. But if we didn't (tell them) they would some day know. So they know they were 'chosen' because they know we love them more than anyone else in the whole wide world." The story of the adoption is made into a myth of origin, implying that the parents chose the child out of all others. In a social-work-approved version, the parents chose the child after the agency had judged that they would suit the child. The myth is primarily, as one parent put it, "to take the sting out of an unpleasant situation."

Revelation, coupled with a tendency toward "rejection-of-difference" is bound to make the adopter hesitant and uncertain as to the explanation he should make to the child: "Adults accept adoption well but seem to find it difficult to explain to their children in a comfortable way. This is upsetting for the children." But the parent's difficulties are not solely caused by the child's immaturity: "There are the feelings about explaining to the child early about adoption, particularly a very small child so that he learns it first from us. There is the fear of confusing him and also involved is the wish that we really were his parents." Understandably, in such circumstances the adopter will seek to remove the image of the natural parents, by avoiding reference to them or by depersonalizing them: "We feel we are the *real* parents and we refer to the (original parents) as 'the lady and the man who had you.'" It is not surprisng that the removal of the natural parents leads to difficulties in dealing with the meaning of adoption. It is, after all, but the reverse of relinquishment. Only he can be adopted whom another has relinquished through death or through some problems of life. Among the latter is birth out of wedlock.

Furthermore, by denying the existence of the original parents the adopters attempt to avoid discussion of the social and personal problems that made the child available for adoption in the first place. But these problems remain to plague the adoptive parents, for they must wonder in what context the revelation about the adoptive status is to be made to the adopted child:

> Would it be possible for suggestions or thoughts relating to the answers we shall be called upon to give our children as they grow up, in connection with their natural parents? We are somewhat apprehensive about this.
>
> We are not quite sure how to answer our children's questions (when they arise) concerning their background—why they were given up, brothers, sisters, family, etc.
>
> There is the problem of how much to tell the child about the child's natural parents—should he ever know about his being born out of wedlock?
>
> Are parents going to tell the children the complete truth about their (natural) parents or will they make up a story which will please the child?

The adopter who wishes to define his own role as that of the true parent figure, can remove the natural parent by the invention of a myth: "We were very elated that our daughter accepted us as Mother and Father from the very first day she came to live with us. She was three and a half years old and we believe that *she was meant for us* and that God had a hand in bringing us together." (Emphasis added.) In this version of the myth of fate where the child is seen not only as chosen but also as fated for the adoptive family, the child is viewed as cooperating with the parent by acknowledging the situation created by the myth. She "accepts the adoptive parents from the first" as if to say: "Of course, we really were meant for each other—even I know it." It has been suggested that myths of origin in the adoptive situation serve as aids in the drive for integration. In this connection we recall Malinowski's observation (1924, 126) concerning the function of myth in Trobriand culture: "It is clear that myth functions especially where there is a sociological strain, . . . unquestionably where profound historical changes have taken place." The adoptive situation certainly contains such strain, inherent in the parents' role handicap, and it arises from the situational discrepancies of childlessness, which represent changes in the life histories of marriage partners. The changes are profound ones because they are unexpected and unprepared for.

The final and ultimate "rejection-of-difference" mechanism found is that of repression or forgetting: "We are telling our daughter she is adopted, but it is hard for us to realize this ourselves. We feel almost as though we were telling her an untruth." Such "forgetting" closes the gap between myth and reality. The myth sustains at the beginning and supports through certain crises. But later the continuous confrontation with troublesome reality is most conveniently avoided by obliterating this reality from the awareness.

PATTERNS SUGGESTING "ACKNOWLEDGMENT-OF-DIFFERENCE"

Although there is a commonly understood term "adopted child," the complementary term "adopter" or "adoptive parent," while used in professional literature, is not in common usage. When we hear people, including adopters, refer to adoptive parents, such references tend to be made to "the Browns, who have an adopted child" or to "the Smiths, who have adopted a child." In other words, for adoptive parents there exists no common symbolic referent to suggest the nature of their adoptive identity and parental role. In the vernacular they are identifiable solely by reference to the *means* of substitute parental role gratification, that is, *having adopted*, or to the ends of gratification, the child. It is as if a teacher's role were not identifiable by the term "teacher" but only by the activity in which he is engaged—"the man who teaches"—or by the social objects he deals with—"the man who has students." This phenomenon is illustrated by the fact that several organizations in Southern California have, for over a decade, used the name "Adopted Children's Association" even though the members are adoptive parents rather than adopted persons. That adoptive parents seek to have their adoptive status recognized in public use is suggested by the appearance of an "Adoptive Parents' Committee" in New York several years after the "Adopted Children's Association" was formed.

Beyond legal adoption itself, institutional mechanisms of the "acknowledgment-of-difference" type do not exist at present. This lack has been deplored by a number of adoptive parents:

> When we went through with the legal adoption at the court . . . we felt . . . that it was a very cut and dried affair.
>
> The formal court proceedings at the legal adoption were disappointing in that there was nothing ceremonious involved.
>
> At Probate Court at the time of completion of the adoption a more meaningful ceremony would be desirable.
>
> In the case of any child old enough to understand what's happening at the time of legal adoption, we feel very keenly that there should be some small ceremony of pronouncing the new family "man, woman, and child." . . . Our adoption day was somewhat of a let-down to the child, perhaps because the judge was so brusque

and brief—too matter-of-fact—unfeeling—or maybe just too busy and too tired.

One agency recently instituted a "termination meeting" with groups of adoptive parents just before they go to court for the legalization. These meetings evidently have a festive character and seem to approach what some adopters have asked for.

The adoption of older children, beyond infancy, involves special difficulties. A five-year-old girl was placed in the home of adopting parents who wanted the child immediately to take their name. The child objected, a fact the new parents found hard to understand. Here the child forced acknowledgment of difference onto the parents.

Adopters can affirm their position as adoptive parents by taking children whose appearance and background betray the fact of their adoption. During the last two decades, a number of adoptive familes have become publicly known for the fact that their adoptions were made across racial lines. Perhaps the best known of these is the family of Carl and Helen Doss (Doss, 1954). In Canada there exists an association of adoptive familes with children of mixed racial background, dedicated to helping find adoptive homes for the many unplaced children of minority ancestry. The association is the Open Door Society.[2]

Alternative to fending off inquiries about the child's antecedents, the adopters can anticipate the kinds of questions which are of interest to others and the matters which can or cannot be revealed. Once anticipated, they can make announcements and other explanations of the coming of an adopted child in such a manner that certain questions are obviated and others are answered.

> Herb and Kay Johnson are pleased to announce the arrival of their chosen son, Howard Andrew
> *Toronto Globe and Mail,* July 18, 1960

2. Open Door Society, 5 Weredale Park, Westmount, Quebec.

Some families have invented other means of educating their families and friends "... we gathered all our nephews and nieces together—gave them a bit of a party—then told them simultaneously of a new cousin they would be having, with his name, showed them his clothes, etc. *We then discussed how important it was that they receive him just as one of themselves.*" (Emphasis added.)

One adoptive mother reports: "We never discuss the individual family history of any one child, but we don't mind saying that most adopted children are born out of wedlock." Another mother says that some of her friends gave her a baby "shower" before she got her first child by adoption. The occasion made it possible for her to tell her friends something about the problems which she and her husband faced in becoming adoptive parents, and what the experience meant to them.

"Evangelism-Recruitment" represents a special kind of education on the positive values of adoption. The adoptive parents' freely expressed enthusiasm or the observed success of an adoption may persuade others to adopt. Adoptive parents' successes in recruiting, enables the potential adopter to see himself as an "instructor" or pioneer.

> We urge people who have love and want children to adopt them.
>
> Three friends with adopted children were very eager for us to find a child to adopt.

Successful evangelism or recruitment also permits the adopters to view with pride the achievement aspect of their status:

> We have several friends who, because of the success of our adopttion, have become adoptive parents.
>
> We were very happy and pleased when a couple, who were childless, decided to adopt after seeing how happy we were with our little girl.
>
> We feel our little girl has been one of the best advertisements for adoption as we have had numerous calls from interested parties, mostly strangers, wanting to know all about it.

Some adoptive parents have intimate contact with other adoptive couples, a fact which probably supplies them with considerable support for their roles: "We know several other couples who have adopted children and feel the same as we do. It is a wonderful feeling to talk about and share the pleasures and problems of children with someone who feels as we do." During the past two or three decades associations of adoptive couples have been formed in various parts of the United States and Canada. Originally concerned primarily with the improvement of adoption legislation and services, they have also come to be important aids in providing role supports for their members:

> We discussed adoption before we were married—neither of us having any idea that we couldn't bear children. We were married about three and one half years before we actively tried to adopt. For the first few years we kept it a secret that we wanted to adopt. After we started telling everyone it became easier to get our little girl. We don't care who knows she's adopted or what they think.
>
> We are charter members of the Adopted Children's Association. We belonged to this organization for a year before we became parents. We are also members of an adopted babies club—eight mothers and their adopted children meet to play every two weeks. . . . We feel that this is good play experience as well as *good for the mothers and children to know adoption together.* (Emphasis added.)

This statement seems important in several respects. The couple had, their story shows, actually considered adoption prior to having a particular need based on known inability to bear children, but only when they were able to divulge their adoption plans to others did they find a child to adopt. They were part of a sample of independent adopters from California. Such people must depend on the help of physicians or, ultimately, of their friends, who may know of an unmarried pregnant woman or of some other situation which would make a child available for adoption. Thus we see "acknowledgment" of *intended* adoptive parental status to be useful in the search for a child without recourse to an agency. The fact that these people, who, in imagination, had tried out the role of adoptive parents long before their actual adoption need arose, had nevertheless at first attempted to conceal that need when it did arise, gives us a clue to another important aspect of our hypothetical typology. The mechanisms of "rejection-of-difference" and "acknowledgment" are most likely *not* mutually exclusive but will be practiced in conjunction with each other. If the activities here identified as part of "acknowledgment-of-difference" patterns of coping are only in their infancy, we must expect that they are not a clear consciously practiced alternative, in opposition to a more established set of role supports. It is more reasonable to assume that, as the situation of child adoption becomes generally known and understood, more coping patterns of the "acknowledgment" type will be employed, and to the extent that this takes place, the role definition of adoptive parenthood will become clearer and thus more satisfactory for those to whom it applies. Two other aspects of these California respondents' statements bear particular attention. This couple had been members of the association for a year prior to becoming parents. For such preadoptive couples, especially those who are not applicants to social agencies, the association serves as a place to air their questions, receive assurance from others who have gone through the experience, and learn how to avoid certain legal pitfalls. At the same time there are social activities which permit the adoptive parents and children to "know adoption together," wherein we recognize the essential aspects of a membership group.

Coping with role handicap by "acknowledgment-of-difference" poses the problem of how to give the child, to whom the fact of adoption has been revealed, a sense of continuity: "(We need) help in supplying a child with a sense of continuity when his hereditary background *cannot* be revealed to him. (P.S. We have found no down to earth answer in the latest publication—small helps, but none pertinent to the 'biggest problem.')" Celebration of adoption as an annual event, which helps provide such a sense of continuity for the child, is practically unknown among adoptive parents. In the 1958 interview study of 70 adoptive parents, only ten indicated that they kept such an anniversary in their families. Among the 283 adoptive couples answering the 1961 questionnaire, no more than 32 said that they had ever celebrated the day. A celebration of this sort may be taken as an "acknowledgment" alternative to the "rejection" oriented myth of origin (*i.e.*, the chosen baby). One may quite properly raise the objection that both the "chosen baby" story and the celebration of adoption share aspects of "rejection-of-difference" and of "acknowledgment." Why then should they be contrasted here? The decision to do so was based on this observation: Telling a story like *The Chosen Baby* (Wasson, 1950) is primarily, as one of the questionnaire respondents said, "to take the sting out of an unpleasant situation"; it acts as a palliative for the adoptive parents' role handicap. The celebration of an adoption day, on the other hand, serves not so much as a palliative as to recognize socially an existing situation, thereby emphasizing that the participants in this family group now belong together.

Unless the adoptive parents have knowledge of these parents the image of the natural parents cannot very well enter the adoptive situation. Confronting the dilemma of ignorance vs. knowledge of the child's background, adoptive parents must therefore be ready to choose knowledge. Such knowledge is more immediate when there has been a personal encounter:

> Met mother before adoption. Experienced sense of assurance.
>
> The unwed mother of the first child came to us and told us she would like to have us adopt her baby. Pleased with the prospect of getting a baby and being selected by the natural mother.

In order to secure the privacy of the new families being created by adoption, the practices of adoption agencies usually preclude such personal meetings between natural and adoptive parents. Nevertheless, there can be links between the two, as this questionnaire entry shows:

> It was important to us to know how the original mother felt about her baby and about letting it out for adoption. She expressed all this in a letter to the agency and they gave us a copy. It was a wonderful letter and we will be glad to show it to our adopted child if and when the need arises for her to know about her original mother. *It gave us an insight into her attitude and created a bond of understanding between us though we never met each other.* (Emphasis added.)

This adoptive mother speaks of her development of insight into the original parent and of a bond of understanding with the natural parent. A communication of this sort creating a common bond of feeling and concern makes it possible for the adoptive parents to introduce the natural parent also into the life of the child. The letter stands as a document of intention and its meaning concerning the act of separation is readily conveyed to the child. Thus, although such an introduction cannot of course remove all problems for the child, it may help to give the child a focus for thought about his first mother and thereby allow him to incorporate something concrete about her into his life picture. A variation of this mechanism was also reported. One adoptive couple hired a pregnant unmarried girl as a mother's helper. The girl's condition, which was not hidden, allowed the adopted child in the family to discuss the meaning of birth, of unmarried mother status, and the girl's subsequent problem of relinquishment of the child. It gave the child the opportunity to think in concrete terms about her own background. Seeing the good relationship which existed between her adoptive parents and the woman who shared their home, she was able to ask them whether her own first mother had been at all like this friendly person.

Empathy is the ability of one person to sense the feelings and needs of another. Empathic orientation toward the child's natural parents thus implies a preliminary "acknowledgment-of-difference." By such an orientation, the original parents enter the constellation of the new family, if only in the adopters' imagination:

> Felt very sad for the unwed mother who had to give up the child, although by this unfortunate experience we were made very happy in being able to adopt a child.
>
> Mother came to this town for the birth of the child. Enjoyed knowing the mother for six weeks. Mother left immediately after birth. But in knowing her have felt sorry for her loss of the child whom she does not know.
>
> I felt a little uneasy about the natural mother parting with such a lovable baby and worried that she might be unhappy.

These reports are meant to illustrate the underlying principle of "acknowledgment-of-difference," and are not to be taken as applicable to all adoptive situations.

In the follow-up interviews with 70 adoptive parents who had originally replied to the mail questionnaire, the question was asked: "Have you ever found yourself trying to imagine how your child feels about being adopted?" Thirty-five of these seventy parents said that they had done so. The parent who orients himself empathically toward the child's special situation thereby acknowledges tacitly a difference in his own parental role from that of biological parents. At the same time he helps himself to overcome his role handicap by anticipating his child's needs.

Of the 1,479 mail questionnaire respondents who reported on the item, "How lucky you are that you didn't have to go through all the trouble of pregnancy and birth like I had," one-third said that it had happened occasionally or frequently. Many of these indicated how they felt when it happened, saying that they were either surprised, embarrassed, annoyed, or upset. In addition, some respondents commented as follows:

> This makes me a little unhappy as I would love to have been pregnant. It is usually said as though I deliberately avoided the discomfort—and as though adoption were very easy.

Little do they realize the birth pangs we experienced in adoption.

It's the hard way if you ask me until the adoption is final.

We waited 28 months for our first child. She only waited 9.

To us that would have been the easy way.

Mental anguish during adoptive period can be tougher than a period of physical pain.

Such comments indicate that the adopters in question were able to recall their relative deprivation preceding adoption, and to that extent they acknowledge the difference inherent in their situation.

Instances of relative satisfaction were of two types. In the first, the adopters compare their parental status with the continuing childlessness of others:

A number of older women (aged sixty or seventy) have expressed envy that adoption was difficult at the time they should have had a child—I of course *felt very lucky.* (Emphasis added.)

We feel fortunate that (we) were able to adopt children; we know many couples who have tried but were unable to.

The second type of relative satisfaction mentioned in the unsolicited material of the mail questionnaire compares the current situation of adoption with the preadoptive period of childlessness:

An adopted child brings so much joy, happiness to a childless couple.

We would like to have had a chance to indicate how very fortunate we are to have had children this way when it appeared we would not otherwise have had children.

The experience of bringing home your chosen child—and to know that he belongs to you—is a rare thrill. We are grateful to the people who have made it possible for folks like us to find children and humble too that we were considered worthy of the names mother and father.

The adopters who are originally without role models will be

aided in dealing with their role handicap if they can find that others are in the same boat. Willingness to recognize such role companions implies some degree of "acknowledgment-of-difference."

> Wife has an adopted cousin, many friends, and her brother has adopted daughter so whole family was familiar with adoption and pleased.
>
> Father is custodian at High School and there are four children adopted belonging to families of the staff.
>
> We were much surprised at the number of people we know or meet who are adoptive parents or adopted children. *We feel very good about them.* (Emphasis added.)
>
> Perhaps the nature of the community matters. We live in a neighborhood where there are a lot of adoptions, and we feel this may ease possible future problems for our daughter.

In the last example the adopters recognize that the presence of role companions for them also provides role companionship for their child. One adopted girl of five asked her parents whether she was the only adopted child in the whole world. She seemed greatly reassured when told that there were many others like her. A young married woman of twenty-two, who had been adopted in infancy, reported in an interview that three or four of her intimate childhood friends had been adopted. She said that when she first discovered this, and throughout her growing years, it was a great comfort to her.

In this review and analysis we have imputed two types of coping function to various patterns of parental behavior. Although among 23 such presumed coping patterns 14 were typed as "acknowledgment-of-difference," this proportion does not mean that it is the preferred mode of adaptation to the role handicap of adoptive parenthood. We also recall here that this hypothetical ordering of behavior by two "pure" types does not preclude their joint appearance in practice. Observation of actual parental behavior suggests that such "mixed" coping is rather typical. The realistic question is therefore in which direction a particular family leans and what this bias means for their collective life. The kind of consequences to be expected from different modes of coping[3] will be spelled out in a theory of adoptive relations.

3. For a summary of coping mechanisms see Appendix D, p. 182.

CHAPTER FIVE

*

Who Copes How?

*

RESEARCH frequently turns up unanticipated findings. At times such findings become strategic for the progress of the investigation. This happened in the case of a student research team[1] engaged in the analysis of unstructured material from the 1956 mail questionnaire. The reader will recall that the questionnaire contained a page on which the participants were invited to enter their own comments. It was among these comments that the coping mechanisms of "rejection-of-difference" and "acknowledgment-of-difference" were first discerned. Such statements as "I feel there is no difference between adoption and natural parenthood" recurred frequently, especially in the case of people who pointed out that they were biological *and* adoptive parents. Among these fecund adopters were those who had had one or more children by birth before they adopted (B-A), and there were others who

1. See p. xi for Overview of Studies in the Adoption Research Project, 1955-1958 (Cynberg, *et al.*, 1958).

had first adopted and subsequently had one or more children by birth (A-B). One of the members[2] of the student research team had noticed that there seemed to be a qualitative difference between the comments made by (B-A) and (A-B) adopters. This student reasoned that the sequence of adoption-then-birth was indicative of greater deprivation than the sequence of birth-then-adoption, since adopters in the former category had originally considered themselves nonfecund. Regarding statements like "adoption is not different from natural parenthood" as indicating defensiveness, she hypothesized that the more deprived adopters (A-B) would be the more defensive. Encouraged to test this seemingly cogent hypothesis, the student selected for analysis the group which claimed to see or feel no difference between adoption and natural parenthood. She counted the number of respondents who mentioned that they were both biological *and* adoptive parents, Investigating each questionnaire to determine which came first, adoptive or natural parenthood, she then noted the proportions of B-A and A-B adopters who said they felt or saw no difference between adoption and natural parenthood. Her counts indicated that while only 20 per cent of the B-A group made such references to adoption, 70 per cent of those in the A-B category did so. What she seemed to have demonstrated was that the more deprived group seemed indeed more inclined to rely on coping by "rejection-of-difference."

Although this preliminary test lacked certain checks, the results were so intriguing that they called for a careful reanalysis of the data, as was subsequently done. First, all the cases which were in any way ambiguous, or where information was inadequate were removed from the total group of those who said "adoption is no different." This inspection reduced the number of cases in both the B-A and the A-B groups by about one-third. The number of B-A cases had been 226; inspection reduced it

2. Elena Reiskind Kruger, second-year social work student at McGill University.

to 141 or 62 per cent of the orignal. There had been 159 A-B cases, which became 100 or 63 per cent of the original number. This fact of reductions of almost identical proportions in the two groups suggested that similar factors had been at work in them, making for the same degree of ambiguity in the data. The remaining cases could now be compared with greater confidence.

The next question was how many of these remaining 241 adoptive couples spontaneously mentioned that they were both adoptive and natural parents ("dual parental position"). Of the 141 B-A adopters, 49 or 35 per cent made such mention and of 100 A-B adopters 32 did so. Thus, nearly the same proportions of the two groups made spontaneous mention of their dual parental position. Finally, and we now reach the core of our study, of those mentioning their dual parental position, how many in each group said they saw nothing to distinguish adoption from natural parenthood? Of 49 B-A adopters who mentioned their dual parental position, 17 or 35 per cent indicated their belief that adoption is not different from natural parenthood, while of 32 A-B adopters 21 or 66 per cent expressed this view. Thus, among the more deprived fecund adopters (A-B) the proportion of those rejecting differences is almost twice as large as that of the less deprived (B-A) parents. While these findings are somewhat less impressive than those from the first test, they are still compelling enough to confirm the hypothesis that the more deprived of the fecund adopters were also more likely to be defensive.

Our question then became whether this relationship between the degree of deprivation and the manner of coping could be shown to hold for nonfecund adopters also. One index of deprivation which makes possible the identification of degrees of deprivation is that of the nonfecund couple's period of childlessness, that is, the number of years which elapsed between their marriage and the arrival of the first adopted child in their home. It may be argued that this is a rather crude index of deprivation; after all, not all couples want children within the same period after marriage. But since more refined data are not available, we will have to make do with what we have. We therefore propose to take the period of childlessness as indicative of the degree of the couple's original deprivation, and the size of their adoptive family as an objective indicator of their adaptation to handicap. We accordingly found that the longer the couple's period of childlessness, the more likely that theirs will remain a one-child adoptive family. Thus, of 487 nonfecund couples who had been childless for less than eight years, 32 per cent adopted only one child. Of 352 couples who had been childless for at least eight but less than twelve years, 41 per cent had adopted only one child. Finally, of 211 nonfecund couples who had been childless for 12 or more years, 55 per cent had adopted only one child. But these figures told us little beyond the obvious. We do not have to wait for our critic to observe that this is probably the relationship to be expected of all family growth. The longer couples wait to have children, the older they get; and the older they are when first becoming parents, the smaller their families will be. If that is correct for biological families, it is so also for many adoptive families, since adoption agencies typically set age limits beyond which a couple cannot adopt an infant. No doubt then that the number of children adopted is not a very satisfactory index of the adopters' orientation to adoptive parenthood.

Fortunately a better index became available to us. This index derives from a study conducted in 1960; four of the five voluntary agencies which had sent out the mail questionnaire in 1956 participated in the study.[3] It had become necessary to learn something about the couples who had not responded to the mail questionnaire. Were they in some way different from those who had responded? The agencies made available nonidentifiable (anonymous) information about these couples—their

3. The Executive Director of the Spence-Chapin Adoption Service indicated that the Board did not permit further participation in our study.

ages, the period between marriage and the first adoption, income, etc.—all data by which respondents and nonrespondents could be compared. Since the project office had a record of the numbers given these cases originally and since the identification numbers of the respondents were at hand, the nonrespondents could be easily recognized. It was in this way that information was obtained about nonrespondents as well as respondents, concerning the number of children they had adopted, and the length of time they had been childless before adoption.

The mail questionnaire had been sent out plainly marked *Adoption Research Project;* it therefore presented the adoptive parents with a minimum cue to the recognition of their parental position. It was argued that response to the questionnaire implied "acknowledgment-of-difference," and that nonresponse therefore represented an index of "rejection-of-difference." Though our previous index had shortcomings, we were curious to see whether it bore any relationship to the index represented by response to the questionnaire. The following figures refer to nonfecund adopters who had taken their child between the beginning of 1950 and the end of 1954. Of 421 couples who had adopted one child, 38 per cent responded. Of 547 who had taken two children, 61 per cent responded. Of 62 couples who had taken three or more children, 77 per cent responded to the questionnaire. Thus the more children the couple had adopted, the more likely they were to answer the questionnaire. In the sense in which we are thinking of response, we can say that couples with more than one adopted child were significantly more committed to the picture of themselves as adoptive parents than were their peers with only one adopted child. This relationship between the number of children adopted and the rate of the response to the 1956 mail questionnaire might have been obtained by chance, seeing that the adopters of 1953 and 1954 had, of course, less opportunity to adopt than the group which took their children in 1950 and 1951. Table 5 shows us that the relationship between number of children adopted and response to the questionnaire is practically the same in each of the five years.

Table 5
Relationship between the Number of Children Adopted by Nonfecund Couples* and Their Rate of Response to the 1956 Mail Questionnaire (Shown Separately for Each of Five Years 1950-1954)

Year During Which First Child Was Adopted	*Number of Children Adopted*	*Total Number of Couples*	*Per Cent Responding to Mail Questionnaire*
1950	1	(74)	29
	2	(79)	54
	3	(10)	60
1951	1	(78)	31
	2	(96)	55
	3	(10)	90
1952	1	(76)	43
	2	(119)	63
	3	(19)	74
1953	1	(91)	34
	2	(128)	60
	3	(11)	82
1954	1	(102)	52
	2	(125)	68
	3	(12)	83

* Includes couples who were nonfecund at first adoption but became fecund later.

We can now feel relatively confident that the response rate is an index of the degree of involvement in the adoptive parental role. With this assurance, let us see what relationship exists between the degree of deprivation, as measured by the period of childlessness, and the degree of "acknowledgment-of-difference" as measured by the rate of response to the mail questionnaire. Of 487 nonfecund couples who remained childless for less than eight years, 59 per cent responded to the questionnaire. Of 352 couples who were childless for at least eight but less than twelve years, 52 per cent answered the mail questionnaire. Finally, of 211 couples who were childless for 12 or more years only 40 per cent responded. Substantiating our student's creative hunch, these percentages show that the greater the deprivation the couple has suffered in childlessness, the less likely they are to respond to the symbol of adoptive parenthood as it was presented in the mail questionnaire. We can now speak about the degree of deprivation, both among fecund and nonfecund adopters, as being related to their manner of coping with the resulting handicap.

It appears then that the greater the deprivation the greater the likelihood that the role-handicapped party will be oriented toward "rejection-of-difference" rather than toward "acknowledgment-of-difference." In the next chapter we can finally formulate a theory of adoptive relations.

CHAPTER SIX

*

Parental Aspirations in Conflict and Harmony

*

IN previous chapters we sought to lay the groundwork for a theory of adoptive relations. To this end we assembled the main points of distinction between the situations of biological and adoptive parenthood. Subsequently, we observed the operation of public sentiments which so often emphasizes these contrasts. From there we identified certain dilemmas confronting adoptive parents in the course of child rearing. It became clear to us that adoptive parenthood is fraught with handicaps with which the adopters must somehow learn to cope. This is how we came to discern certain patterns of behavior to which we ascribed coping functions. Finally we noted that the greater the deprivation suffered, the greater the likelihood that coping would take the form of "rejection-of-difference."

However, we must now introduce a further question. It concerns the relative utility of the patterns of "rejection-of-difference" and of "acknowledgment-of-difference" as alternative means of coping with role handicap. But no satisfactory answer can be given to such a question until attention has been paid to the nature of parental goals. The question of the relative utility of different ways of coping must then be posed along the following line: *Given certain generally applicable goals for parenthood, which of the two patterns ("rejection-of-difference" or "acknowledgment-of-difference") is likely to be more useful in coping with role handicap?*

When the relationship between ends and means is relatively straightforward we should expect little difficulty in making such an analysis. Thus, when a physically handicapped man seeks to cover a certain amount of distance, as crossing a street, the relative utility of an artificial leg as compared with a wheel chair can be fairly readily assessed. However, if his main goal is conceived not so much in his getting across streets as in the maintenance and enhancement of his sense of adequacy and dignity, the problem of what means to choose in pursuit of these ends has been greatly complicated. How is one to gauge the relative efficacy of certain acts as means of furthering so imponderable a goal as "personal adequacy" or "dignity"? Parental goals may be similarly imponderable.

GOALS OF PARENTHOOD

The marital bond and the ensuing family group are meant to be permanent among us, irrespective of the reality of a high divorce rate. This is made evident by public reaction a few years ago to the statement attributed to the famous debutante, Gloria Vanderbilt just before her marriage at age 17 or 18 to Leopold Stokowski. When she was interviewed for a national magazine and asked how she felt about her coming marriage, she is said to have replied that she felt very happy about it, and that first marriages are so romantic. Miss Vanderbilt certainly did *not* seem to be looking forward to the permanence of her marriage. She may have been expecting a more matter-of-fact, less romantic one, to follow it. Students who were asked how they regarded this statement attributed to Miss Vanderbilt have uniformly indicated that they detested it, showing that they considered such a view of marriage outside the established rules. Many of these same students also agreed to the propriety of divorce, but only as a last resort, not as a goal of equal strength with the maintenance of the marital relationship and family group.

The view of marriage attributed to Gloria Vanderbilt provides the needed contrast between the cultural norms regulating marriage and behavior that deviates from these norms. What is laid down in unwritten or written social rules is made manifest in the sentiments and overt behavior of people. The likes and aversions expressed by many members of a society are indicative of that society's rules, for it is in the nature of human beings to desire what is held socially necessary. We may regard it as a safe axiom to say that couples entering marriage generally expect *theirs* to be a reasonably happy one, capable of standing the test of time and circumstances. We may further assume that in looking forward to the coming of children, they expect *their* family group to be relatively harmonious and stable. Such goals of permanence, stability, and harmony are essential as long as the family is the setting in which children enter the stream of social life. If the day ever comes when statements like the one attributed to Miss Vanderbilt reflect a wide agreement concerning desirable goals for marriage, it will mean that the family as we know it has come to an end.

In thinking of stability as a generally applicable goal for family life, we have to consider the ever-present reality of change. Children become ill, get into scrapes, and grow up to leave home. Fathers have disappointments in their occupations; even so happy an occasion as a promotion may result in a serious dislocation of the family's life pattern. After any such upheaval people are sometimes heard to say, "I'm glad we can settle down again" or "It's good to be getting back to normal." But such remarks do not necessarily herald a return to the previously known situation. Rather they suggest that the current situation is becoming familiar, and that one is beginning to act in it with competence. Stability as a family goal thus implies not a static state of affairs but rather "dynamic stability," the assumption that a certain degree of change is normal and that it will be followed by a new sense of equilibrium. In summary then, we shall regard parental goals principally to involve the following: (1) harmonious relations yielding personal satisfactions; (2) dynamic stability of the family as a group; and (3) the group's permanence.

Adoptive parents may be taken to be no different from biological parents in their aspirations for family life, with perhaps one exception. For adopters the attainment of stability and permanence may loom even more important and pressing than for their biological counterparts, who have not been equally deprived and who thus do not have the same sense of uncertainty. Among the three parental goals (which are undoubtedly not exclusive ones) we may safely assume that adoptive parents most strongly seek stability and permanence.

MEANS SUITABLE TO THE FURTHERANCE OF FAMILY STABILITY AND PERMANENCE

We must now identify the means which are most likely to fulfill the parental goals of family stability and permanence. Families are groups and in a larger sense we are asking what makes groups of people stay together. This general question cannot be answered within the limitation of our chapter and a definitive answer, covering all types of groups and all circumstances, cannot be given. However, in general outline one can say that group stability and permanence require: (1) the existence of common interests among the members; (2) rules of conduct regulating their behavior; and (3) some agreement on which members of the group have authority in the administration of the rules.

Families are special kinds of groups. The parent members come together first; in modern marriages they come together by mutual choice and consent. But children do not join the group of their own volition, be that in the typical family by birth, or the less typical one involving the adoption of infants or young children. (When older children are adopted beyond a certain age, their consent is needed. Such family groups are clearly quite different in this respect.) In the early phases of biological and adoptive family life the relationship between parents and children is bound to be an unequal one. To begin with at least, the administration of rules clearly rests with the parents. They are the family authorities. The nature of this authority, how it is divided among the marital pair, who has jurisdiction over what aspects of family activty, the relative strength and weakness of the power they wield, the nature and extent and clarity of the rules which they administer, even the interests which the family members pursue together, depend to a considerable degree on the kind of society, the time and place, of which the family is a part. In colonial America, the number of interests which pressed families into common action was far larger than in our own day. For instance, educating children, making clothes, or growing food fell much more into the immediate daily round of the colonial family than into ours, which for all these tasks tends to depend on outside services. Thus, there are fewer occasions forcing members of modern families to spend time in common endeavors.

Besides, in colonial America, as in many other preindustrial societies past and present, the rules of conduct regulating the behavior of family members were laid down in customs derived from tradition. These traditional rules had the considerable merit of being applicable in like situations. Thus the conduct expected of children at meal times or the activities of women in their households were probably quite similarly understood in Provincetown and in Philadelphia. Furthermore, the way power was allocated in the administration of family rules was also traditionally determined. Considerations of age and sex were important criteria in the traditional allocation of power in families. The modern family cannot rely on such clarity of role definition. Traditional family patterns are less and less in evidence, being especially noticeable in relation to rules of conduct and allocation of the power needed for the administration of rules. Whatver may have been the practice of bedtime for children in colonial Provincetown or Philadelphia, many of us know from intimate experience that bedtime rules are quite chaotic among us. Each family has to make its own and these are frequently modified, not on bases of best parental judgment, but because power is usurped by children who manipulate their parents with the aid of stories about late bedtimes in the houses of neighborhood children. Parents give in because it is easier, because they themselves are unsure of their authority, or because they think it may not, after all, be so important. They also may be under the impression that they are carrying on democratically, when actually they are avoiding their responsibilty of maintaining order in the family.

We have here been thinking about families as groups and what gives them a relative stability and permanence. Where traditional rules and traditional authority arrangements are weak or altogether lacking, what is to take their place to keep the family a going concern? The answer has to be of the order of an educated guess rather than reliable knowledge. The couple will probably have to bring to the marriage, or develop in it, certain skills of relationship to serve them as substitutes for traditional rules and traditional authority arrangements. Some rules for the regulation of conduct there must be, and some authority in the administration of the rules is also essential for dynamic stability and group permanence.

Rules, if not given, must be made up by the group. This is a function of leadership, and parents represent the natural leaders in family groups. Parent leaders must choose among a multiplicity of contending patterns governing the allocation of power in the family. Whether the roles they choose will involve traditional power arrangements or quite different ones depends largely on them. We see then that on both counts the married pair must be relatively inventive. The ability to invent or to choose rationally among various alternate rules and roles depends, it seems, on another skill. This is the ability of the married pair to communicate to each other regularly the observations that they are making about their common situation of marriage and family. This communication skill has two interconnected aspects. The first is the ability of the partners to sense what is going on in the other member. The second communication ability concerns ideas. The weaker the traditional rules for the control of behavior in the family, the more the stability of the family group depends on the members' awareness of what is the pertinent, the necessary, activity at a certain moment. The more critical the circumstances at that moment, the more important that the members correctly discern the nature of their predicament and that they correctly estimate the most applicable means of acting within it. What they discern and consider the necessary behavior for members of their family group they must be able to communicate to each other. Thus they will have to have some facility with ideas and the expression of ideas. After a family crisis it doesn't do much good to say, "I thought of something that would have helped us, if you had known it too." The idea must be communicated before or at least during the crisis. In summary we may say then that we regard certain skills as essential means for furthering the goals of dynamic stability and permanence of the family group where traditional rules are relatively weak. We judge that at first the parental pair, and eventually they and their children, must be inventive in making and administering rules. We judge further that this disposition is facilitated by communicative skills on the level of feelings (empathy) and ideas.

THOUGHTS ABOUT THE RELATIVE UTILITY OF DIFFERENT COPING PATTERNS

What assets and liabilities can we theoretically attribute to the two coping patterns? At the beginning of the parent-child relationship in adoption, the parents will most likely seek to find their main gratification in the enjoyment of the child's presence. Having been long deprived of children, the very fact of their attainment of the new parental status is itself deeply satisfying. It is no surprise then to find the couple eager to immerse themselves thoroughly in the parental experience and anxious to ward off any thoughts or actions which might impede the full enjoyment of it. In other words, patterns of "rejection-of-difference" will prove the most satisfying mode of accommodation for the new adoptive parents. These patterns tend to soothe old feelings of hurt and to provide compensation for the months or years of deprivation preceding the adoption. With these patterns of coping one can "forget the adoption" and live just like any other parent. "Telling a story that will please the child," will also please the adoptive parents in that, for them, it "takes the sting out of an unpleasant reality." On the asset side, we note that "rejection-of-difference" aids the adopters in moving into parenthood, in feeling that the child is theirs.

But children grow and their world expands. The time inevitably comes when the child, who has been told of his adoption, will ask why he was given up in the first place. When that happens, a soothing story may not so readily satisfy the child, and the parents' previous reliance on patterns of "rejection-of-difference" may make it difficult for them to shift to more realistic means of accommodation. Also, it seems reasonable to suppose that reliance on "rejection-of-difference" tends to inhibit the inventive and communicative skills we regarded as necessary for the fulfillment of adoptive parental aspirations when there is little traditional support. This conclusion seems plausible because by practicing "rejection-of-difference" the parents insulate themselves against recall of their alienation and pain of the preadoptive period, and against the present impact of disenchantment. In circumstances of enchantment one does not need to stay alerted against difficulties, for all will "turn out right in the end." The anesthetizing practices of "rejection-of-difference" are likely to desensitize the parent against the inchoate, inarticulate ways in which children are known to broach to adults their problems of understanding difficult concepts. If the parents feel that, for them, certain aspects of the subject of adoption are threatening, they obviously cannot readily deal with ideas and feelings that arise for the child as a result of his knowledge that he was adopted. In such circumstances the child is likely to feel that the door to communication with the parents is closed. Accordingly he will ask few questions and those he asks will be tame. If this happens, the parents may assume that there are no problems, when in reality the child is being isolated from them. Such an isolation would seem the doom of the long-run aspirations the parents have for their relationship with the child. We are therefore inclined to think that, whereas "rejection-of-difference" patterns may make for initial gratification, they will be liabilities for the adoptive relationship in the long run. We believe that only acknowledgment of the realities involved in adoption is capable of fostering the delayed gratification that comes from the realization of having helped to build an adoptive relationship of strength and durability. These considerations now lead to the following hypothesis:

> If adoptive parents put their main emphasis on patterns of "rejection-of-difference," they will tend to close those channels of communication with their child which we believe are essential for the stability of a family type that lacks traditional supports.

If, on the other hand, adoptive parents put their main emphasis on "acknowledgment-of-difference," they will more likely keep the channels of communication open, and will thereby enhance their own long-run satisfactions.

A FIRST TEST OF THE HYPOTHESIS

In this chapter we shall want to formulate our total theory and are therefore eager for a preliminary test of our key hypothesis. Such a test is possible with the aid of information from a questionnaire interview study of 70 adoptive parents. These parents had answered the 1956 mail questionnaire, so that considerable information from them was already available. When they were interviewed in 1958, the main object of the study was to ascertain whether the "rejection-of-difference" and "acknowledgment-of-difference" concepts could be further validated. The subsequent analysis of these interviews furnished opportunities for a test of our hypothesis.

The hypothesis has made use of the four concepts: (1) "acknowledgment-of-difference"; (2) "rejection-of-difference"; (3) "communication"; and (4) "satisfaction." These concepts have to be translated into measurable units for purposes of analysis. We now turn to the answers the adopters have given to interview questions. The questions themselves represent our concept indicators. For instance a question like this: "Do you feel that biological parents have satisfactions that adoptive parents don't have?" is taken to indicate the respondent's orientation toward "rejection-of-difference" and toward "acknowledgment." Because "rejection-of-difference" is simply the opposite of "acknowledgment-of-difference" we shall here think of it as an extreme pole in a continuum of attitudes toward difference. We shall refer to indices of "acknowledgment-of-difference" by which we will try to measure the degree of that attitude expressed by a particular parent. Accordingly, registering a low degree of "acknowledgment" means that the respondent tends toward "rejection-of-difference," at least as measured by that index.

Some of the indices we shall use are made up of several questions or items. These will be known as scores. Because of their complexity and length, the scores are referred to only by name in the text. They are shown in detail in Appendix B. Some single questions also serve as indices. Such questions will always be shown in the text or in the statistical table in which they have been employed.

The correlations between indices will suggest the relationships that exist between different parental attitudes. For instance, we shall inquire whether the capacity for empathic communication is more likely to appear in combination with "rejection-of-difference" or with "acknowledgment-of-difference." In Table 6 we find that only 24 per cent of the adopters who deny that natural parents have special satisfactions ever imagine how the child feels about being adopted. But of the adopters who acknowledge that natural parents have special satisfactions, 68 per cent say they sometimes imagine how the child feels. Our reasoning is therefore along lines of probability. We see that "acknowledgment-of-difference" is more likely to be related to empathic communication than is "rejection-of-difference." Although different indices are employed, Tables 7 and 8 show that the same relationship obtains between "acknowledgment-of-difference" and empathy.

Table 6
Relationship between Type of Parental Coping Activity and Empathy with Adopted Child

		INDEX OF COPING ACTIVITY Q: Do you feel that other parents have satisfactions that adoptive parents don't have?	
INDEX OF EMPATHY		A: No (Rejection) *(N = 25)*	Yes (Acknowledgment *(N = 31)*
Q: Have you ever found yourself trying to imagine how your child feels about being adopted?	A: No	76%	32%
	Yes	24%	68%

Table 7
Relationship between Type of Parental Coping Activity and Empathy with Adopted Child

		INDEX OF COPING ACTIVITY Q: Do you feel that you (your wife) have missed an important experience (in not bearing children)? A: No (Rejection) (N = 25)	Yes (Acknowledgment) (N = 37)
INDEX OF EMPATHY			
Empathy Score	Low (0-3)	72%	43%
	High (4-6)	28%	57%

Table 8
Relationship between Type of Coping Activity and Empathy with Adopted Child

		INDEX OF COPING ACTIVITY "Acknowledgment-of-Difference" (A-D) Score		
		Low 0-4 (N = 20)	Medium 5-7 (N = 26)	HIGH 8-14 (N = 24)
INDEX OF EMPATHY				
Empathy Score	Low 0-3	80%	46%	36%
	High 4-6	20%	54%	64%

We have spoken of indices of "communication," which assumes that "communication of ideas" and "empathic communication" are closely related. That this is indeed so, is shown in Table 9. The greater a parent's capacity for empathy, the more likely is he to think about the child's original parents.

Table 9
Relationship between Empathy with the Child and Readiness to Think about the Natural Parents

		EMPATHY SCORE			
		Low 0-2 (N = 15)	Medium 3 (N = 22)	Medium 4 (N = 13)	High 5-6 (N = 20)
INDEX OF COMMUNICATION OF IDEAS					
Q: Now a question about your child's original parents. How often would you say you think about them: frequently, just once in a while, or never?	A: Never	67%	45%	15%	5%
	Once in a while, frequently	33%	55%	85%	95%

Parents admitting that they missed an important experience in not having a child born to them are also more likely to think about the child's original parents. Thus "acknowledgment-of-difference" is more likely than "rejection-of-difference" to be associated with capacity for communication. (See Table 10.)

Table 10
Relationship between Type of Parental Coping Activity and Capacity for Communication about Natural Parents

		INDEX OF COPING ACTIVITY Q: Do you feel that you (your wife) have missed an important experience (in not bearing children)?	
		A: No (Rejection) (N = 25)	Yes (Acknowledgment) (N = 32)
INDEX OF COMMUNICATION Q: Does respondent ever think about child's original parents?	A: No	52%	24%
	Yes	48%	76%

How does the adoptive parent's attitude toward his special situation affect his sense of satisfaction with it? Table 11 shows that the greater the degree of "acknowledgment-of-difference," the more likely it is that the respondent regards his situation to yield special satisfactions.

Table 11
Relationship between Type of Parental Coping Activity and the Experience of Special Satisfaction

		INDICES OF COPING ACTIVITY					
		S-D SCORE			*A-D SCORE**		
		Low (N = 17)	Medium (N = 33)	High (N = 12)	Low (N = 30)	Medium (N = 21)	High (N = 19)
INDEX OF SATISFACTION Q: In your opinion do adoptive parents have some satisfactions which other parents do not have?	A: No	53%	33%	8%	52%	40%	16%
	Yes	47%	67%	92%	48%	60%	84%

* The A-D score contains the question which makes up the Index of satisfaction.

As we would have expected, we also find that the greater the parent's capacity for empathy with the child's situation, the more likely he is to feel a sense of special satisfaction with adoption.

Table 12
Relationship between Empathy with the Child and the Experience of Special Satisfaction

		EMPATHY SCORE		
		Low 0-2 (N = 14)	Medium 3-4 (N = 34)	High 5-6 (N = 20)
INDEX OF SATISFACTION Q: Do adoptive parents have some satisfactions which other parents do not have?	A: No	50%	41%	20%
	Yes	50%	59%	80%

SUMMARY OF FINDINGS

1. A high degree of "acknowledgment-of-difference" is associated with a high degree of empathy with the child (Tables 6, 7, 8).
2. Empathy and communication of ideas are closely related (Table 9).
3. A high degree of "acknowledgment-of-difference" is associated with readiness to think about the child's natural parents (Table 10).
4. The higher the degree of "acknowledgment-of-difference," the more likely that the adopter will feel his situation to be especially satisfying (Table 11).
5. The higher the degree of empathy with the child, the more likely it is that the adopter will feel his situation to be especially satisfying (Table 12).

These statistical relationships support our hypothesis. We can now hold with some degree of confidence that the capacity for communication with the adopted child is enhanced by the parents' readiness to acknowledge the difference between adoption and natural parenthood. But we also wish to know whether good communication between adoptive parents and children actually fosters cohesiveness of the parent-child relationship. Unfortunately, data are currently not available for answering this question with any degree of certainty. However, there is a clinical report by Eleanor Lemon (1959) which suggests that the inability of adoptive parents to communicate with their children on the subject of the natural parents, adversely affects the parent-child relationship. Lemon's cases are pertinent to our inquiry. Some of them are therefore reproduced here.

> The majority of persons who came to (the agency) for help . . . have been adults. Without fail, when it is information about original parents they are seeking, a barrier exists between adoptive parents and child in this intimate area. The parents seemingly have been emotionally unable to accept the fact that the child was not born to them. In the majority of cases the adoptive parents had told the child of his adoption, but had not been able to accompany this with an emotional warmth which would envelop the child *and his background.* There appeared to be a lack of recognition of the child's need to have his curiosity satisfied. There were those who told fictitious stories—usually involving death of one or both parents. The child usually detected the falsity.
>
> A letter from a young married woman who remembered her original father—and pleading for information—clearly states the problem. She says, "I am sure it would break my mother's heart if she thought I still thought about my real parents and family." She goes on to speak of two occasions when she had broached the subject with them—occasioning tears from her mother and questions as to her happiness from her dad. Then she adds, "I was never allowed to talk about my adoption and so as a little girl I thought it was a disgrace to be an adopted child. Now, as I look back, I can see they were striving to get me to forget the past."
>
> One intelligent young woman came to us when about to start her career. *She had learned from the adoptive parents as a small child that she was adopted. There had been no further conversations with them about the matter and she felt completely unable to broach the subject with them.* She felt her father to be a more approachable person than her mother—to whom she had never felt very

close. She spoke of her as an unpredictable person, for whom she actually felt a pity. In looking up her record, we found that she had been a foundling who had been placed at a time when the adoptive mother's disappointment about childlessness had been keenest. Thirteen years later, however, the original mother dared to make herself known to the Society to ask news of her child. The information she gave us was then shared with the adoptive parents, but it was too difficult for them to tell the child. The young woman had reached outside her adoptive home for affectionate relationships. A young couple who had adopted children became her close friends. She spoke also of how her religious faith had helped her love and understand her adoptive parents.

We tried to help this young woman to understand that her adoptive parents' need to think of her as their own had made it difficult for them to tell her about her adoption. She was a person who put an honest effort in trying to see their point of view. We told her how the deprivations of the depression years had caused her original parents to leave her in a place where she would be cared for. Quickly she expressed genuine recognition and appreciation of the material and educational advantages her adoptive parents had given her. *There is real question, however, if she will ever be able to share with them the fact that she knows her story as they do.*

In contrast is the story of another woman, also a foundling, who came to us primarily for help in obtaining a birth certificate. She had with her the clipping from a newspaper telling of the fact that she had been found as an infant in an attended rest-room. *This had been given to her by her adoptive parents.* Though they had not confided in her the fact of adoption until she was a school age child, one felt there was a free-flowing kind of relationship between them. She was not in conflict and was not interested to know if there was more to be learned about her original parents.

The sharing of experiences by the persons interviewed has allowed us insight into *the need of the adopted child to reconcile his identification with two sets of parents.* It has supported the conviction that *it is not enough for adoptive parents to share only the fact of adoption with the child, and to be vague and evasive about original parents.* Curiosity, repressed or overt, and fantasy on the part of the child is a certain outcome—with all that this can mean in interference with the richness of the emotional bond with adoptive parents. Such interference with the free-flowing relationships between parents and child means inevitably some degree of damage to the child's emotional development. (Emphases added.)

Suggestive as Lemon's clinical data are, we have no way of knowing whether they are representative of the experiences of adopted persons. For that, one would have to look beyond the group which comes to an agency to make inquiries. But for the time being, in the absence of other data, these will serve us to feel that our hunch is correct: namely, that good communication between adoptive parents and children is needed for the long-run cohesion between them.

THE THEORY OF ADOPTIVE RELATIONS

We are now in a position to summarize the theoretical argument which has been developed in these six chapters.

1. Childless couples entering upon adoption are confronted with a series of difficulties which we identified as role handicap.
2. This role handicap is reinforced by the attitudes of other people.
3. In the form of parental dilemmas, the role handicap is carried into the evolving family relationship.
4. To cope with their role handicap and feelings of alienation, the adopters take recourse to various supports for their roles. These coping mechanisms appear to be of two types: those which serve the adopters in denying that their situation is different from that of biological parents ("rejection-of-difference"), and those which serve the adopters in acknowledging that difference ("acknowledgment-of-difference").
5. The greater the original deprivation and the consequent role handicap suffered, the greater the likelihood that the adopters will lean toward mechanisms of coping by "rejection-of-difference."
6. For all parents in our society, certain cultural goals may be assumed. There is no doubt that adopters, along with other

parents, seek to have familes of stability and permanence, yielding personal satisfactions. Stability requires rules of conduct. Families that are not regulated by tradition must depend on the interpersonal skills of their members for their internal order. In the situation of adoption, these skills imply empathic and ideational communication with the child about his background.

7. Adoptive parental coping activities of the type of "acknowledgment-of-difference" are conducive to good communication and thus to order and dynamic stability in adoptive families. Coping activities of the type of "rejection-of-difference" on the other hand can be expected to make for poor communication with subsequent disruptive results for the adoptive relationship.

This theory will presently be applied to the question of what adoptive parents can do in a practical way toward strengthening their family life.

CHAPTER SEVEN

*

Pioneer Enterprise

*

IF our theory is to be more than an academic exercise, we must prepare to put it to work. Our first point of application is the cultural script. Can this script be made clearer and less conflicting than it is at present for the adoptive parent actors? As it is now, the adoptive situation is beset with ambiguities. The very fact that in our language no differentiation is made between procreating parents and fostering parents initiates the ambiguity. Language directs thinking. Concepts constitute building blocks of our language and of our actions. Given such lack of the essential symbols one need not wonder at the tendency of people to act on the premises inherent in their language. As long as the actually experienced reality closely approximates the way things "ought to be" according to the language, things will be clear enough for people. But when drastic changes of a physical or social nature make the experienced reality sharply different from what people expect on the basis of their language and ideas, the situation and its constituent parts become ambiguous. How this ambiguity makes itself manifest in the outlook and feelings of the adoptive parents is illustrated in excerpts from two letters by mothers who wrote to a woman's magazine in response to the article, "To My Adopted Daughter—I Wish I Hadn't Told You" (1959).

> The adopted child is no different from any other child. They have the same needs and the same yearnings as any other child. But I will admit that your responsibility is more than the average parents'—it is your responsibility to show the adopted child that there is no difference at all—and it is your attitude toward the adoption that will form your child's thinking.

Like so many of the respondents to our mail questionnaire, this parent claims that there is no difference between the adopted and the natural child. At the same time, the writer suggests that the parent must make a special effort to show the child that there is no difference. If there were no difference in the situation of the two children, the effort would be quite unnecessary, and one suspects that the counsel to make the effort would not have been given. Whence this confusion? Our values are embedded in our language. As Myrdal recalled for us in his epoch-making study of Negro-White relations (Myrdal, 1944), we have a pressing values commitment toward equality of opportunity in our society, while there are also many strains in the opposite direction. The difficulty for this parent writing to the editor arises from the common confusion between the objective description of members of a group and the subjective evaluation of the worth of the members. It is objectively true that there are differences between the children in any family—parents must and do distinguish even between twins. It is quite another matter to differentiate between the children in a family along lines of their intrinsic worth. The confusion of this parent stems, in part at least, from the nature of our values of egalitarianism, for these are ambiguously embedded in our language.

The other letter is a moving human document. The mother writes that she has felt "an affinity with the author: I have, as have my children, experienced most of the things described in the article. This is as far as I am in accord with her." This mother then claims that in her view the "to tell the child" prescription is right but that the psychological experts "didn't give us workable methods." She proceeds to discuss how she deals with the problems raised by "telling":

> Months go by when it isn't even mentioned. When it comes up sometimes, through outside influences, we talk about it. We examine it, then put it away. Like everything else in an orderly life, it has its place. And each time I know that she is building up her confidence, her defense against a part of her life which can be described as unusual, but never undesirable.
>
> The perfect human being has never been born. *We all have some defect that we must learn to live with.* When we have accomplished this, then we have learned to live with the rest of the world. *Being adopted is NOT a defect.* Only in trying to hide it can we create one. Only in believing it to be a secretive thing can we give credence to the undesirability of it." (Emphasis added.)

The correspondent began by showing how she deals with the "telling" in an orderly way and why she believes that her method helps her daughter. She ends that paragraph by asserting that the daughter is helped to form a defense against an unusual (as against an undesirable) part of her life. Such is the nature of language, however, that it leads us to think in the customary modes which are established by words. The mother has used the word "defense" and we are not really accustomed to "defend" ourselves against the unusual so much as against the undesirable. And so she is led to use a term closely related to "undesirable" by making reference to "defect." "We all have some defect," she says, apparently making a connection here with the meaning of adoption for her daughter. And she draws the conclusion that sensible people will simply accept their defects and learn to live with them. But no sooner said and the writer abandons the logic of her proposition. "Adoption is NOT a defect," she says. "Only in trying to hide it can we create one." This mother's problems were the problems of our value conflicts as reflected in our language. She knows that some things have to be wrong before there can be an attempt at rectification of things—here through adoption. So long as we will think in "enchanted" terms of perfection, we must also think of the actual state of man as fraught with defects. And when we do, we will suddenly find ourselves confronted with the fact that we are apparently making invidious distinctions between persons, on the basis of their intrinsic value.

The emotional component of ambiguity in the cultural script is even more poignantly brought home in these paragraphs from the same letter:

> I never minimized my childrens' natural parents. When my daughter said to me once, in anger, "I'll bet my other mommy was prettier than you and better than you," I answered, "I'm sure she was beautiful because you are. I don't know if she was better, but I'll at least admit to the possibility." We both laughed when my daughter said, "You're really not so bad."

This is relaxed "acknowledgment-of-difference." Yet a few paragraphs further she concludes this way:

> As for my children feeling a need to thank me, if ever they feel a sense of obligation, I'll understand. I'll tell them that I'm grateful too; so grateful for the opportunity to give them a heritage, a heritage of strength, a capacity for understanding, and the ability to be happy. If ever I achieve this then I'm the best mother in the world. *I will finally have obliterated those nine months, and everything that came before them.* The future belongs to us, because we belong to each other. (Emphasis added.)

There is no need to enlarge on this adoptive mother's ambivalence, her leaning simultaneously toward the opposites of "acknowledgment" of the natural parent in one sentence, and "rejection" through obliteration of the pregnancy in the other sentence. Nor does her ambivalence take away from the greatness of this document. If our correspondent is inconsistent, the cause is to be found less in her than in the ambiguities inherent in our values and in our language.

Language conveys the content of the cultural script. Actors who have at their disposal a script with conflicting directions cannot very well be expected to put on a consistent performance. The foregoing letters illustrate the behavior of actors whose script is ambiguous and which therefore represents a poor guide to the roles to be played in the drama.

Let us briefly recall the conflict in the cues which the script of this culture provides adopting parents. Prior to adoption they have experienced deprivations having physical as well as cultural implications. By adopting, the couple hope to compensate for these deprivations. Having set out on the venture, they find that this step, which promises to be so real and so satisfying to them personally, after all does not make their parental position or role expectation the full equivalent of the position or role expectation of biological parents. The cultural cues on the one hand *invite* people to adopt if they cannot otherwise satisfy the urge for parenthood. These positive cues are inherent in the growing interest and publicity given adoption in recent decades. But opposite cues are also present. These enter a variety of circumstances. There are the legal and administrative impediments to easy adoption which give prior right to consanguine relationships until these are permanently ruptured. Through such impediments, adopters become indeed "petitioners" for parenthood. Among the cues with a certain amount of negative valence is the increasing pressure on couples to adopt through licensed agencies. Initially at least, this procedure tends to emphasize, rather than to diminish, the adopters' dependency in the process of obtaining a child. Dependency represents a form of punishment for people for whom relative independence is a central value.

These particular cues belong to the start of the drama of adoption. Others continue on into later acts, as for instance in encounters with inquisitive outsiders, whereby the substitutive nature of the adoptive relationship is emphasized. But adopters are themselves instrumental in conveying ambiguous cues to one another. The following note was attached to a questionnaire, filled out in a group meeting of adoptive parents:

> Even in this group tonight people refer to children natural born to them as "our own" and to the others as "adopted." I feel my two children are "my own." Am I too touchy?

COPING WITH AMBIGUITY

We have been thinking about the preadoptive experience of nonfecund couples in terms of failure to meet the dominant ideal of biological parenthood. This view leads to the question of the meaning of "failure" in our culture. We know that "success" is itself a central goal; this is illustrated in a common saying like "nothing succeeds like success." By this standard, failure in a venture that is culturally defined as important tends to reflect negatively on the adequacy of the person who has failed. One aspect of this cultural condition is the "sense of failure." By the very fact of his membership in the society or group upholding the success standard, the person who has failed *feels* himself to be a failure. He feels that he is powerless to cope with his situation on his own. Since "success" is the goal, failure to reach the goal implies a lack of power to control one's own destiny. A sense of failure is thereby also a sense of powerlessness.

There are several ways in which one can meet this situation. One of these is to turn against one's own goal, to disclaim it, perhaps to choose an alternative which may be within reach. As the fox in Aesop's fables, one says to the world and to oneself, "I really didn't want those grapes that much." Another approach is to acknowledge the goal and, by accepting its standard of success, to devalue oneself. That is patently destructive. It is possible, however, to accept the goal and to maintain one's sense of dignity.[1] This may be done within a group of others who have been similarly handicapped and who also seek support in their plight. Such a group represents a

1. Riesman (1954) has proposed another response which he calls "the nerve of failure." It implies not only "the ability to face the possibility of failure," but also the "assumption that past and present failures need not mark the limits of human power." This view represents a philosopher's ideal answer to failure. It recognizes failure for what it is, holding it lightly in the perspective of the history of human efforts. Since, however, it is not given to every man to be a philosopher and to accept failure with equanimity, on his own, it seems reasonable enough for him to look to a collectivity for an answer.

source of substitute power. It not only protects the members from being overwhelmed by a sense of failure, but provides a setting for mutual aid. In the company of others who can appreciate the meaning of one's experience, because they have had similar ones, there is the opportunity to gain new powers.

Another adoptive mother's response to the magazine article defines both the lack of power and the group approach to its recovery:

> I read with great interest the article in the September [issue] entitled "To My Adopted Daughter—I Wish I Hadn't Told You" by Henrietta Sloane Whitmore. Here at last is an article on adoption that gets past infancy.
>
> It motivated me to return to my notes on the growing up processes of my children. For I too am an adopted mother; my son being past eighteen and my daughter fourteen. And my husband and I, even as Mr. and Mrs. Whitmore, must face approaching adulthood of these young people with very little to guide us.
>
> But I depart from the conclusion Mrs. Whitmore draws. While our experience is parallel to a degree, I cannot accept the capsule "to tell or not to tell" as a remedy for any part of this problem. I do have a plan which has a far broader reach and could help Mrs. Whitmore, and me, and every other parent in or contemplating adoption. . . .
>
> Mrs. Randall Smith (pseudonym)

The magazine's editor had given permission to contact any of the correspondents. Mrs. Smith's letter suggested a follow-up. We therefore wrote to ask about this plan of hers. Here is the pertinent part of her reply:

> I have found too much of technique, and not enough of practique. Through all the years of progressive schooling and parlor and professional psychoanalyzing, it became apparent that nobody really knew anything at all about adoption. The words and music went "you are chosen, tra la la," period. The psychiatrists we went to readily admitted to no experience and could only discuss the problem in terms known to them. The only comfort came in talking to other adoptive parents, and we couldn't help each other too much because our children were more or less the same age. For the parents of the younger children I was the expert. But I needed

to talk to parents of *grown* adopted children—or to the grown adopted people themselves. How? Where?

> Part of my plan was a sort of Adoptive Parents Anonymous—where we could communicate on all age levels, older and younger. All existing studies and articles on adoption seemed limited to the process itself. Nowhere could I find anything on the dynamics of adoption; the continually spiralling evolvement. I'd like to have had a sort of Gesell on adoption to help me anticipate the developmental lines—not to be followed as a road map but rather to be used as a compass or direction finder. I don't know how much of a plan this is for your purposes, but I know a dozen adoptive parents who get understanding only from each other.

Mrs. Smith's plan calls for a group in which members can communicate on all levels of their experience. Through such communication, members with less experience could be helped to anticipate future events, on the basis of the knowledge gathered by members with more experience. Such knowledge, if it is correct, implies that the members to whom it comes vicariously can face their situation with more confidence. Under such circumstances knowledge means power.

The utility of groups in situations of uncertainty has been noted by a number of investigators. The following summary statements are Klein's (1956, 88-89).

> When there is no group whose norms are perceived as relevant in an unfamiliar situation, the norms of the culture will determine the behaviour of the individual. Conversely, firm attachment to the norms of a group will enable a member to ignore or go against the norms of the culture.

(For us this means that adoptive parents can most effectively develop new norms and resist the cultural norms which are inappropriate to their own situation, if they are attached to a group of people with similar interests.)

> In situations of uncertainty, the information afforded by the group will be responsible for the individual's behaviour.

(The parent group can give information to those about to be initiated into adoption on what to expect and how to deal with the new situation. It will therefore serve to supply role models to guide new adopters in establishing appropriate behavior.)

> The individual will tend to estimate success within the limits and of the kind approved by the group to which he seeks to conform.

(If the parent group can set up standards of success for adoptive parenthood, the adoptive parent can begin to evaluate himself by these standards rather than by those of the culture and its fecundity values.)

Mrs. Smith has referred to the group she envisaged as similar to Alcoholics Anonymous. She has thereby implicitly recognized that such a group would supply help in the situation of failure and powerlessness—in short, a situation of role handicap. Klein would agree with her: The group supplies alternate standards to those which are inappropriate or harmful, and it gives information and support in place of uncertainty and insecurity.

SELF-HELP ASSOCIATIONS AS A REALITY

Associations of adoptive couples have existed for some time: The Adopted Children's Association of Los Angeles was founded in 1948; the Adoptive Parents' Committee of New York came into being about a decade later. What do they consider their purposes to be and what benefits are actually derived by the membership? We are interested in these groups precisely because we feel that they might offer clues to the ways in which adoptive parents can solve some of the problems related to adoption. It will be recalled that membership in parent groups was hypothetically placed in the "acknowledgment-of-difference" pattern. There were indications that the Adopted Children's Associations are oriented toward mutual aid. For some years, the folders describing the Los Angeles and Whittier associations read in part:

> (The Adopted Children's Association) is . . . composed of civic-minded men and women *who have banded together* for the purpose of *pooling individual experiences into a common force* to help

provide love and security through *solid family ties* for every child who is adopted or who needs a home. . . . (Emphases added.)

The intent of the "banding together" is then the "pooling of experiences" which, it is hoped, will advance the parental goal of "solid family ties" which in turn provide the personal gratification of "love and security." Other purposes of the groups were announced to involve the improvement of "California adoption laws, long considered inadequate" and aiding in the interpreta· tion of adoption to the community.

These organizational goals might be summed up as concerned with three areas of mutual interest: (1) Provision and extension of friendly contacts between people in the same boat. (2) Extension of legal protection for the "boat" and its occupants. (3) Increased public understanding of the "journey." For the sociologist these goals are suggestive of particular kinds of groups, typical of heterogeneous societies claiming adherence to a systhem of egalitarian values. Such "minority groups" are categories of people who experience certain kinds of social deprivations because of physical or social characteristics they share. Members of minorities frequently organize mutual aid groups. One such group, the National Association for the Advancement of Colored People (N.A.A.C.P.) has long carried on the struggle for the implementation of the constitutional rights of the Negro minority. It will prove instructive to compare here the stated purposes of the N.A.A.C.P. with those of the Adoptive Parents' Committee of New York (A.P.C.).

N.A.A.C.P.	A.P.C.
To educate America to accord full rights and opportunities to Negroes.	To give accurate and timely information on adoption matters.
To fight injustice in the courts when based on race prejudice.	To investigate and publicize injustices in adoption procedures.
To pass protective legislation in state and nation and to defeat discriminatory bills.	Constantly advocate remedial legislation at all levels of government.
To secure the vote for Negroes and teach its proper use.	Cooperate with existing agencies toward broadening their policies, thus freeing more children for adoption.

To stimulate the cultural life of Negroes.	**Consider problems of mutual interest among adoptive families.**
To stop lynching.	

There is an obvious affinity between the goals of the two groups. At first sight, the N.A.A.C.P. and A.P.C. goals under the fourth point appear unrelated; but when we ask ourselves what the "vote" means for Negroes and "availability of children" for would-be adoptive parents, the basic similarity is evident in the provision of the power to meet ultimate group goals. Throughout there is a remarkable parallelism between the stated goals of these two otherwise quite different groups. This parallelism can be understood in terms of the common factor of minority group organizations. That these goals are not merely announced but are worked for can be seen by an inspection of their activities. Organizations like the N.A.A.C.P. and the American Jewish Congress have thus fought, and scored signal victories, against official procedures that aid discriminatory practices. A 1961 issue of the newsletter of the Los Angeles Adopted Children's Association makes reference to an "education committee" which had begun to investigate "entrance blanks in the different school areas to see if upon entering your child in school, you have to write if your child is a natural or adopted child."

Minority group organizations typically aim at providing greater equality of opportunity for their members. They therefore tend to exhibit an inherent conflict between the maintenance of a separate identity (given by the very fact of their organization) and the processes of assimilation to the dominant group (typified by the struggle for equality). Intensive study of the Whittier Adopted Children's Association and observation of similar organizations suggest that this conflict does apply. Thus, among the monthly programs of the Whittier association in 1959 and 1960, only a small proportion provided opportunities for "pooling of individual experiences." The study also showed that couples tended to join just prior to or at the time of getting their first child and that they tended to let their membership lapse after two or three years. The association appeared to attract mostly couples in need of first models for the roles of adoptive parenthood. But even such early models were apparently thought to serve essentially assimilatory interests. A newspaper release about the tenth anniversary of the Whittier Adopted Children's Association defines it as "a group of parents, relatives or persons concerned with adoption. *By sharing common experiences they are able to give their adopted child a beginning like that of a child born to natural parents.*"[2] (Emphasis added.) This statement has been called assimilatory because it suggests that association membership leads to the capacity for creating the semblance of a biological parent-child relationship. Here the formal organization has given public expression to the dilemmas of Enchantment vs. Disenchantment and Integration vs. Differentiation.

ADOPTIVE RELATIONS AND THE SOCIAL PSYCHOLOGY OF MINORITY GROUPS

The role dilemmas faced by adoptive parents and the organizational dilemmas of their associations can be better understood when viewed in the light the genus "minority group." Kurt Lewin, in several of his essays on the characteristics of minority group membership, asked how Jews in America could best meet the then growing threats to their sense of security and their sense of worth. He was writing at the time of the rise of the Nazi terror; he himself was a German Jewish refugee. Lewin's answer, in short, was to suggest that Jews accept their minority group position and that they make it a position of strength. In one essay (1940, 43-45), he dealt with the problem which Jewish parents face in bringing up their children in an inhospitable world. He understood that the Jewish child's greatest need was for solid social and psychic "ground" on which to stand. Although the problem of the Jewish minority situation is in some respects quite unlike that of adoption, the final para-

2. *The Whittier News,* March 15, 1961.

graphs from this essay of Lewin's bear a striking resemblance to what we have concluded about adoptive relations:

> In regard to the Jewish problem the action of Jewish parents should be the same as in matters of sex or any other education, namely, *true, open, and realistic.* These are the considerations to act on:
>
> 1. The basic fact that their child is going to be a member of a less privileged minority group, and he will have to face this fact.
> 2. The attempt to keep this problem away from the child as long as possible, and soft pedal it, will in all likelihood make for greater difficulties later on.
> 3. This applies just as much in a community where the child is so fortunate as not to encounter anti-Semitic difficulties in his early life; parents should realize that the problem is bound to arise at some time, and the sooner it is faced, the better.
> 4. Such an early build-up of a clear and positive feeling of belongingness to the Jewish group is one of the few effective things that Jewish parents can do for the later happiness of their children. In this way parents can minimize the ambiguity and the tension inherent in the situation of the Jewish minority group, and thus counteract various forms of maladjustment resulting therefrom.
> 5. Outstanding among the techniques that parents should employ is the treatment of Jewish problems not as an individual and private matter but as a social issue. For instance, to press the child harder for good behavior, or to raise his personal ambitions higher than is customary in the Gentile majority, puts the child merely in a state of keener tension that makes for less easy adaptation. Parents should from the very beginning stress the social aspect of the situation. This is more realistic and helps to prevent the personal uncertainty and self-accusation or self-pity which otherwise are the results of anti-Semitic experiences.
> 6. A better understanding of the sociological problems involved is of particular value to the Jewish adolescent. For it can help him to solve one of the most bewildering puzzles, . . . what kind of a group the Jews are (i.e., a religious group, or a nationality, or a race), whether he personally belongs to them. He will often feel himself more like some Gentile friends than like some Jews, and he is apt to make this feeling of similarity or dissimilarity his measuring-stick for group belongingness. It is true that some sociologists have made one or another kind of

similarity between members the defining mark of a group. However, similarity between persons merely permits their classification, their subsumption under the same abstract concept, whereas belonging to the same social group means concrete, dynamic interrelation between persons. A husband, a wife, and a baby are less similar to each other, in spite of their being a strong natural group, than the baby is to other babies, or the husband to other men, or the wife to other women. Strong and well-organized groups, far from being fully homogeneous, are bound to contain a variety of different sub-groups and individuals. It is not similarity or dissimilarity that decides whether two individuals belong to the same or different groups, but *social interaction or other types of interdependence.* A group is best defined as *a dynamic whole based on interdependence rather than on similarity.*

7. Parents should not be afraid of so-called "double allegiance." Belonging to more than one overlapping group is natural and necessary for everyone. The real danger lies in standing "nowhere"—in being a "marginal man," an "eternal adolescent."

The similarity between the situation of the Jewish and the adoptive parent-child relationship was not lost on Lewin. In the essay from which we have quoted, he referred to the adoptee's need to know about his adoption as a parallel to the Jewish child's need for knowledge concerning his Jewishness. We shall presently have occasion to deal with some of Lewin's rules for minority parenthood. Meanwhile, let us take note of an important *dissimilarity* between the minority situation of the adoptive family and that of other minority group families. In the Jewish and the Negro family, both parents ordinarily share with the child characteristics on which the social stigmas of minority group status are based. The racial, ethnic, or religious minority family is therefore a microcosm of the larger minority group. Its members will find common interests through their very interdependence of fate. This interdependence is less readily given in adoption where there is no larger natural group beyond the family. Besides, it is relatively rare for adoptive parents themselves to have been adopted. Under such circumstances, how are adoptive parents to advance this interdependence within their families? The answer is suggested by much of our previous thinking here. It would seem impossible for adoptive parents to create a real interdependence unless they can convincingly relate their own fate to the child's. The adopted child's fate, however, involves the totality of his background. To create an interdependence of fate in the adoptive family, the parents must therefore come to accept the totality of the child's background. None of it must be alien to their values or their views of themselves. This means that adoptive parents must be able to identify themselves with the natural parents. If they cannot do so, the child will most likely come to sense the distance which exists between them and his forebears. This in turn will mean that the adoptee will find it difficult or impossible to fuse the images of his natural and his adoptive parents into a single configuration, one which is acceptable and satisfying to him. Such considerations suggest that adoptive parents must cast their lot in with the adopted child's, and that they must do so without mental reservations.

How are adoptive parents to approach this necessity; what does it take for them to be able to cast in their lot wholeheartedly with their child's? To answer this question, let us briefly look once more at the way in which adoptive parents are currently inclined to deal with their child's lot and theirs. A recent self-survey of the membership of the Barker Foundation, a licensed adoption agency organized and controlled by adoptive parents, indicates that for this group, ". . . most children are between six and eight years old before adoption has a conventional meaning. Most parents whose children are seven and over report that their children 'understand what is meant by adoption.' . . ." However, the report goes on to say: "One-half of the parents whose children are seven or over report having talked with the children about the biological parents." These parents understand that between the years of six and eight their children are ready for an expanding knowledge of their situation.

On the other hand, only half of these same parents whose children are in that age group have talked about the biological parents. The report also says:

> It is clear that ultimately an interpretation of adoption involves some discussion of the birth parents, but generally this discussion does not arise until the child has achieved a fairly high degree of maturity, at least until he is ten or over.
>
> Most adoptive parents feel that adopted children should have virtually no information about their biological parents during early childhood, but should know anything that they want to in their adulthood. There is considerable diversity of opinion as to how much should be known during adolescence.

Whence this hesitancy? The Barker report provides a possible answer:

> One of the problems of major concern to the adoptive parents is the interpretation of the marital status of the biological parents. Ninety-two per cent of the adoptive parents responding to the questionnaire have not told their children whether the natural parents were married or unmarried. *Many adoptive parents make specific note of this area as one in which they would like some specific help.*" (Emphasis added.)

This hesitancy may then be assumed to stem from the forces which we discussed earlier as the third of the adoptive parental dilemmas. A recent unpublished report from Great Britain indicates that it is a widely applicable dilemma. In this report, Iris Goodacre found that among the factors which made parents delay an explanation of adoption was of course the matter of the child's age, but also,

> diffidence about explaining the facts of life, and the related problem of explaining illegitimacy. There were few adopters who could bring themselves to tackle this latter problem of their own accord: The three children who are aware of their illegitimate origin each were thought to have been enlightened about this aspect of their history by others outside the family circle, before the matter was discussed and explained by the adopters.
>
> A problem for the more discerning adopters was their wish to be

loyal to the child's parents—to avoid for the child's sake saying anything too detrimental. Yet they were at least equally anxious that there should be no occasion for even a hint of divided loyalties. More than one adoptive mother was obviously concerned about the prospect of telling the child that his mother was unmarried, and the problem of explaining that the mother had not wished to keep the child appeared at least equally formidable, though in a different way. The possibility in the child's mind of being the "best baby" which was how they were informed they were chosen, and the reconciliation of this with having been the baby that was not wanted, was a problem for deferral.

The Barker and Goodacre reports and our own observations coincide in suggesting that adoptive parents have difficulties in reconciling themselves to the out-of-wedlock origins of their children. They may consider the revelation to represent an overwhelming difficulty for the child. Eleanor Lemon's study suggests that they are wrong in this:

> The question is often raised if the fact of illegitimacy is not harder for the adopted person to accept than legitimacy. We have not found it to be so. On the contrary, it was often an expected and certainly a more easily accepted reason for his parents to have given him up. Sometimes the sensitivity about illegitimacy is more with the person who is interpreting the circumstances than with the person so born. The story of a bright little five-year-old boy comes to mind. One day an anxious adoptive mother telephoned to ask advice about what she should say next to her son. He had been plying her with questions as to why his mother had given him up. She had answered him many times with the story that the lady to whom he had been born had loved him but that because she could not make a home for him she had wanted him to have her for his mother and father. She began to wonder if this answer was completely satisfying for him since he asked so often. One day he again asked the question and while she was anxiously searching for a better way to explain it to him, he said, "Oh, relax mother—I know—she was an unmarried mother!" She realized that he had recently overheard a conversation on the subject of unmarried mothers. We encouraged her in the acceptance of his explanation—since children's attitudes grow to be a reflection of our own. As his understanding develops, her own compassion

will help him in the acceptance of the particular circumstances of his birth (Lemon, 1959, 46).

Adoptive parents may also be afraid to broach the subject of illegitimacy because they do not want to make the child feel separated from them. Perhaps adoptive parents want to feel that their fate and the child's are inseparably linked. Most of the adoptive parents cannot objectively share the child's fate of having been born out of wedlock. But there exists the possibility of sharing that fate vicariously. This, however, can be done only by parents who have sorted out their own feelings and ideas concerning the meanings of legitimacy and illegitimacy. At present, there is much ambiguity surrounding these concepts. The writings of sociologist Kingsley Davis (1939) can assist in this task of clarification. Some of his ideas have here been abstracted and combined with ours.

Some Sociological Considerations Concerning Illegitimacy

All known societies require children to be born into a family of some kind. In nearly all societies there is the expectation that a mother and a father will receive the new-born. This is necessary not only for reasons of protection and support, but more so for reasons of orderly reckoning of descent and unambiguous family relations. In spite of the universality of such reproductive norms, children are not exclusively born in wedlock. To help explain why out-of-wedlock births occur more or less frequently in this society, we may want to consider the following:

1. In spite of the fact that there are moral rules as well as laws against fornication, there are innumerable conditions in this society which actually induce people to break these rules. What is more important, these conditions are frequently sanctioned. It is thus not surprising that a certain number of people will fail to satisfy the sexual code of premarital continence or intramarital sex relations.

2. People are not given equal access to information about and training in birth control methods, so that some people are

less likely than others to escape the consequences of having disobeyed the rules of sexual conduct.

3. Further, there are mores and laws against abortion so that it is not possible with a clear conscience to terminate a pregnancy artificially, once it has begun.

These are some of the conditions which explain why the reproductive norms, which bid people to bear their children only in wedlock, are not consistently obeyed.

Such an explanation stresses the sociological rather than the personal problems involved in out-of-wedlock birth. It makes clear that children should be born into families, for only so can descent be reckoned without ambiguity. Furthermore, the hostility directed toward the bastard child results from the fact that the reproductive norms have been thoroughly institutionalized. If we really wanted to change the feelings directed toward the child born out of wedlock, we would have to change the social institutions which now require birth within marriage only. It is these institutions which make for the abhorrence of bastardy.

These reasons suggest why, for children born outside the protection of a family, a substitute family is desirable. If the natural parents can marry without duress and legitimate their child, this may be best. If they can not, and in order that the child shall have a father as well as a mother, adoption by people other than the biological mother or her kinfolk may well be the less confusing and disruptive solution. This line of reasoning makes the necessity of adoption understandable.

Such an explanation furthermore helps the adoptive parents in coping with the dilemma of how to teach sexual and reproductive norms without slandering the biological parents. First of all, with the perspective of social and cultural factors as part of the explanation of why children are sometimes born outside of marriage, there is no need to attach blame to the natural parents. We had previously indicated our belief that the adoptive parents must be able to identify themselves fully with the child's natural parents if they wish to be able to throw in their lot with the adopted child. This they can do only, it would appear, if they can make clear to themselves, and to the child, that there but for the grace of fortuitious and more fortunate circumstances go they. In other words, they must be convinced that their own more legitimate situation makes them not one whit more virtuous than the child's natural parents. The child, however, must be given training in maximum responsibility for the maintenance of the reproductive norms. How is the adoptive parent to accomplish this?

There are two types of sexual norms, each of which leads to similar goals of reproduction within marriage only. The first of these norms is absolutist, it insists on abstinence from sexual relations except in marriage. It is based on romantic as well as religious considerations, reminiscent of an ideology of enchantment in which life is seen as a thread of unbroken, evolving state of being. The second of these sexual norms is relativistic. It may be called a sexual ethic of consequences, since it seeks to control people not by reference to absolute prescriptions and proscriptions, but by posing the question: "What will be the outcome of this act?" Once "outcome" is put into a context of social relations, it becomes an ethic of responsibility for the welfare of others. The ethic asks: "What will be the result of this act for all the parties involved?" In a sexual relationship outside of marriage such a question involves, of course, the possible offspring from the union. With proper knowledge and care, conception may be avoided. There are, of course, other issues to be considered. Given the current norms, sex relations outside of marriage may take a serious psychic toll of the partners. A sexual ethic of responsibility is thus only a partial guide to satisfactory conduct. Being based on rationality rather than tradition, it is a disenchanted code.

Once we have this view of two possible sexual codes, each meant to lead to births within marriage only, we can see a possible answer to the reduction of the adoptive parental dilemma which we have discussed here. As long as adoptive parents are personally committed to teaching the *absolutist* ethic of premarital sexual chastity, they cannot logically avoid the implication that the child's natural parents are to be blamed for the act which led to the child's birth. Only if the adopters can give their allegiance to a sexual ethic of responsibility can they do otherwise. Even this will not be easy, but they can point out that men and women must under all circumstances consider the consequences of their acts for the well-being of all parties concerned. Then, on the basis of our previous considerations regarding illegitimacy, they can note that circumstances sometimes make this so difficult that people fail.

It may be argued that such an ethic would induce the adopted child to identify himself with the natural parents to such an extent as to repeat the pattern himself. Jolowicz (1946) showed some years ago that this kind of "self-fulfilling prophecy" is likely to occur when the foster parent maligns or otherwise rejects the child's biological parents, and not when the biological parent is accepted. It would seem then that by making the child easy about the event of illegitimacy through removing the element of blame from it, the child may also effectively be protected from becoming victimized or victimizing others in his or her own sexual life.

If these views are accepted as correct, it follows that adoptive parents with absolutist sexual ethics will feel restrained from fully throwing in their lot with that of an adopted child who was born of unmarried parents. Indeed, such adopters are likely to see the adoption in part as an "uplift" or "salvage" operation, a circumstance which does not allow for a thorough interdependence of fate.[3] It also follows that adoptive parents who are

3. Social work agencies and the courts which have responsibility, respectively, for the establishment and confirmation of adoptive relations may want to institute some inquiries into the wisdom of allowing children born out of wedlock to be adopted by couples who adhere to fundamentalist or other rigid religious norms. It may be that such couples would make otherwise good adoptive parents, but should be restricted to adopting children

not committed to an absolutist sexual ethic can more readily move toward increasing interdependence of fate with their child.

Implications of Lewin's Views for Adoptive Parenthood
We now return to Lewin's counsel to minority parents. That counsel can be generalized to include the situation of adoption:

1. The minority group child has to face the facts of his life.

2. It is best that these facts are faced squarely from the start, by involving the child in that knowledge.

3. This applies under the best and the worst of minority group circumstances, since the conditions can and do change.

4. The minority parent can thereby set up a situation in which the child has a definite sense of belongingness with other members of the minority situation. This minimizes ambiguity, tension, and maladjustment.

5. Minority parents should treat the minority problem not as an individual and private matter but as a social issue. This will prevent feelings of self-accusation and self-pity which can otherwise result from contemplation of the minority experience.

6. This sociological approach is especially important for the adolescent minority person. He needs to have considerable reassurance concerning his belongingness. This is best provided through the interdependence of members of the minority group. (The adolescent adoptee who, because of his age may be somewhat at odds with his parents, may thus need others in the adopted family with whom he can identify himself, to whom he can feel close. Brothers and sisters provide that opportunity, especially perhaps when one or more of these are adopted. A sense of interdependence among siblings in an adoptive family can provide reassurance concerning belongingness.)

7. Minority parents should not be afraid of overlapping loyalties. (In our case this means that the adoptive parents allow the child to consider his first parents as part of himself, much

with whose background they can more easily identify themselves. There is also the fact that there are now adopters who have a commitment to such values or who are uncertain about them. Such parents might be helped to reorient themselves with the help of individual or group counseling procedures.

as he needs of course to consider his adoptive parents as part of himself.)

Lewin's rules for minority parental conduct thus cover the entire range of our own theoretical formulation for adoption. The application of the Lewinian model came as an afterthought. Its neat fit suggests that the realities of "role handicap" as formulated here and those of "minority group position" and "marginality" are closely related. It suggests further that there may be generic patterns of coping relatively successfully with various and apparently quite different types of handicap.

In this chapter we have seen how the role handicap which derives from lack of clarity about one's role can in part be remedied by inventive steps. Among these steps is the participation with others in self-help activities. Out of such activities may arise greater clarity about the otherwise handicapped role. Further, self-help associations may add to their members' sense of autonomy. The confrontations between the role handicapped and the helping professional can be put on a more fruitful basis in settings where the former feel themselves "at home." Improvement in the conditions of role clarity and autonomy is analogous to the joint tasks that are fostered by frontier circumstances. The hazards of the unexplored area can frequently be dealt with best by cooperative action. Pioneers must be inventive. They must be willing to forswear reliance on previously learned but now inappropriate performances. In adoption this means that the actors must pioneer new avenues to the satisfactions of parenthood. How they can approach that task will be the subject of a later chapter.

The ambiguities and contradictions which drastic change tends to bring are probably not all reducible by rational action. In the following chapter we shall explore the outlines of such a contradictory, residual phenomenon.

CHAPTER EIGHT

*

Boy or Girl? A Speculative Detour

*

AS surveyors and cartographers we have made a number of educated guesses about unexplored territory, sketched them in and followed them up. We have mainly sought to provide enough topographical detail for pioneers securely to traverse the territory. They would still have to blaze their own trails and help each other build bridges and shelters. In this way they would be able to rectify any errors we may have made and fill in needed details.

Our mapping task is nearly finished now and we are about to supply an interpretation of our topographical findings. Just now, however, our attention is drawn to a peculiar formation which lies toward the edge of our territory. We are tempted to ignore it for it is not likely to interfere directly with trail building. But on a hunch we decide to investigate the formation further. We reason that its outcroppings may tell us something of the subterranean structure of the land. As the rock formation underfoot is unalterable, some knowledge of it may aid the pioneers in the location of their trails.

The phenomenon to which we are referring has been observed by others. For over three decades, it has been noted that adopters seemed to have a preference for girls. Why would these observers remark on it unless they considered the phenomenon in some way peculiar, unless they saw it in contrast with the desires of potentially fecund people? Since we are trying to understand adoptive relations, this phenomenon has to be of interest to us. In this chapter we shall explore whether it is indeed a phenomenon to be taken seriously. Does it recur sufficiently regularly to represent a pattern and can our hunch, that it contrasts with the preferences of fecund people, be substantiated? If the facts are what they are reported to be, we shall then want to inquire into possible meanings of the phenomenon. Our first step then is to marshal the facts.

THE FACTS OF PREFERENCE FOR GIRLS IN ADOPTION

Thirty years ago, Alice Leahy (1933) reported on the characteristics of adoptive parents. During the decade 1918-1928, Minnesota residents adopted 2,414 children who were born out of wedlock. Among a number of other characteristics, Leahy noted that the adopters took girls in preference to boys. Fifty-four per cent of the children adopted were girls. This proportion could of course reflect other factors than a preference on the part of the adopters. It could be that more girls were available for adoption or, if a sizeable proportion of these adopters were related to the children they took, the child's sex would not be a consideration for them. But Leahy has also shown that more boys than girls were available during this period and that nearly 95 per cent of the adopters in question were unrelated to the children they adopted. We are therefore able to agree with Leahy that in the group she studied the adopters seemed indeed to prefer girls.

Colby (1941) collected information on adoptions made in nine states (Alabama, California, Massachusetts, Minnesota, New Mexico, North Dakota, Oregon, Rhode Island, and Wisconsin). Out of a total of 2,041 adoption petitions filed in 1934, 1,206 or 59 per cent were made by nonrelatives. Of this group of non-relative adopters 645 or 54 per cent took girls.

Gordon (1930) assembled the sex ratios of children adopted in various parts of Germany during the 1920's. Two of the 13 figures she gives are here quoted. In 1926-27, the Berlin Red Cross placed 66 children, of whom 66 per cent were girls. During the years 1925-27, the Youth Bureau of the city of Breslau (Silesia) placed 150 children of whom 86 per cent were girls. Following a long list of such figures, Gordon adds the comment that, in contrast with the sex ratio of children placed for adoption, among the children relinquished for adoption there were everywhere about as many boys as girls.

Leahy, Colby, and Gordon inferred a female sex preference among adopters from the sex ratios of adoption petitions or final adoption decrees. In addition to this indirect information, data on manifestly expressed sex preferences are also available. Brenner (1951) studied 50 families who adopted between 1941 and 1945. At the time these couples applied for a child, 39 expressed a sex preference. Twenty-eight of this group or 72 per cent had asked for a girl.

In 1956, the mail questionaire study of the attitudes and experiences of adoptive parents was begun at McGill University. The questionnaire was sent to a sample of their clients by a number of U.S. and Canadian agencies. These clients had received their first child between the beginning of 1950 and the end of 1954. Subsequently, these clients were studied along a number of characteristics for which information was available in the agency records. By this means, sex preference data, as given at the time of application for a first child, were obtained for the adopters in these samples. Of 670 childless couples who expressed a sex preference at the time of application, 308 or

46 per cent asked for a girl. While these figures do not indicate a preference for girls over boys, when the sex preference patterns of the respondents in the McGill study are compared with the sex preferences of people who look to offspring of their own, the adopters were indeed considerably more inclined to want girls. Kornitzer (1952), in speaking of adoptions in England, suggests that the overwhelming preference for girls may be disappearing and explains this fact by the following observations:

> The waiting list for girls is far longer than for boys—or was, for *adopters have now usually heard how difficult it is to get a girl.* (P. 45; emphasis added.)

> Once accepted the applicants have nothing more to do but wait, and they sometimes wait a long time, particularly if they insist on a girl; but *publicity, by making the long waiting lists for girls well known, has helped to shorten them.* (P. 77; emphasis added.)

These observations suggest not so much that the preference patterns have radically changed, but that people will subordinate a secondary goal to a primary one. If a couple assumes that their admission of a preference for a girl may seriously delay, or even ruin their chances of getting a child, they may very well try to hide this preference if it is not so vitally important to them. Another factor may also be involved in reducing the proportion of female preference among more recent groups of adopters. In the earlier decades of this century, the adoptive family was typically a one-child family. But among the nonfecund couples in the 1956 McGill mail questionnaire study, the majority had adopted at least two children. It stands to reason that when one wishes, and is able, to get a second child, the sex preference for the first child will be less pronounced.

Irrespective of these considerations with respect to the McGill data we can summarize our findings by saying that there appears to be a tendency among adoptive parents to prefer girls. The observers whose data were quoted above regarded female sex preference as a characteristic of *adoptive* parents since it is ordinarily said that people want boys when they are having their first child by birth. It would obviously be desirable if we could bring some facts to bear on this pattern believed to be more typical among biological parents. Before moving to an investigation of the meaning of female preference in adoption we shall want to establish the factualness of male preference under conditions of fecundity.

THE FACTS OF MALE SEX PREFERENCE

Evidence for the existence of male sex preference under conditions of assumed fecundity derives from the studies of Neely (1940), Rockwood and Ford (1945), Dinitz, Dynes, and Clarke (1954), and Kirk. Neely's student groups exhibited a decided preference for boys as hypothetical first children. Rockwood and Ford's Cornell student sample responded similarly. Out of 364 students, 156 or 42.6 per cent had no decided sex preference. Of the 208 students who expressed a preference, 197 or 94.7 per cent said they wanted a boy for their first child:

> Many of the 42.6% who mentioned no sex preference added some qualifying comment such as, "Sure, I want a boy, but what's the use of having a preference?" From these remarks it appears that many others actually would prefer their first child to be a boy but have resigned themselves to taking what they get. There was little difference in the preferences expressed by men and women . . . (Rockwood and Ford, 1945, 149).

Dinitz and his co-workers at Ohio State University asked 380 undergraduates about their sex preferences for hypothetical first children. The student respondents were permitted either to express a sex preference or to say that they had none. Of 249 students with a decided sex preference, 92 per cent said they preferred a boy. In 1960 Kirk asked Whittier College students about their preferences for hypothetical first children. Out of 96 students, 80 per cent said they preferred boys as first children.

Feldman and Meyerowitz are currently studying the development of the marital relationship. These investigators have asked 392 married couples, expecting their first child and with the wife five to six months pregnant, what their sex preferences are. Of 312 men with a decided preference, 82 per cent are reported to have wanted a boy. Of 296 women with a decided preference, 59 per cent wanted a boy. There is thus more than folklore in the belief of preferences for a son as a first child when people have no reason to doubt their actual or potential fecundity.

VARIOUS EXPLANATIONS OF DIFFERENTIAL SEX PREFERENCE

The phenomenon of a preponderant male preference in biological family formation as against female preference in family building by adoption is here called "differential sex preference." Earlier we suggested that this phenomenon, if real, might yield insights into the adoptive situation which our previous approaches had missed. But we are not the first to seek to explain the phenomenon. We shall briefly look at some of the explanations that have been proffered to account for differential sex preference.

1. It is less difficult to bring up a girl than a boy (Colby, 1941, 67; Kornitzer, 1952, 169).
2. A girl is seen as a symbol of affection. From a "cuddly" little girl she becomes "companionable" as she grows up, and throughout life, even though married, "stays closer to her parents" than does a son (Brenner, 1951, 39; Kornitzer, 1952, 169; Gordon, 1930, 60).
3. A daughter costs less to raise (Gordon, 1930, 60).
4. A daughter is more of a help in the parental household (Gordon, 1930, 60).
5. It is usually the wife who really presses to adopt and her wish is for a girl (Brenner's term is "narcissistic preference") Gordon, 1930, 60; Brenner, 1951, 39).

6. By choosing a girl, the people with fears about adoption can more readily take a child from some other parentage (Brenner, 1951, 39; Kornitzer, 1952, 169).

While we must agree with Brenner that "the preponderance of requests for girls above boys is something not fully understood," we want to take these hunches, put forward by other students, and put them to whatever tests are at our disposal. The first of these tests is that of logic. Points 1-4 apply equally to biological and adoptive parents and can therefore not serve to account for a difference between them. Points 5 and 6 are specific to adoption. They might be restated as follows:

5a. Women normally provide the driving force toward adoption.
5b. When women have their own way they naturally (or narcissistically) prefer girls.
6. Female preference arises out of a fear of taking, as one's own, a child from another parentage.

In the following paragraphs we shall investigate female sex preference with these suggested explanations as guiding hypotheses.

FEMALE SEX PREFERENCE EXPLORED

Hypothesis 1: Women suffer more from childlessness and are typically the driving force toward adoption.

In Chapter 1 it was shown that women tend to recall their original deprivation of childlessness in more urgent and troubled terms than do their husbands. That this is so is not suprising. Both the biological structure of woman as childbearer and the social roles that have almost universally accrued to her as childrearer make her intensely role handicapped when the capacity to fulfill this pattern is lacking. The fact that occupational pursuits are powerful supports to men's roles and in the majority of instances are only substitutes for women suggests that men can bear a childless state far more readily than women. We are therefore inclined to accept as plausible that part of the hypothesis stating that women are the most deprived, and that the more deprived partly is likely to be the more anxious for compensation through adoption. But what about the part of the hypothesis that states that women, left to their own, to their natural narcissistic wishes, prefer a girl like themselves? Here we must marshal data from previously mentioned studies. We saw that student respondents at Ohio State University and at Whittier College overwhelmingly wanted boys for first children. There was no statistically significant difference between men and women in the frequency of their male preference for first children. But we also need to stop and ask ourselves what it means to make a hypothetical choice for the sex of a *first* child. It implies that there will be more children, that one is not really *very* firmly committed to a male sex choice, that one likes girls too as any good modern parent should! Thus in our view of a "basic" sex choice by women, the more crucial case is that for a hypothetical *only* child. Students at Ohio State and Whittier College were asked about their choice of an only child's sex. The frequencies of preference for a boy as an only child were as follows: At Ohio State University, of 185 men students, 92 per cent said they wanted a boy, and of 195 women students, 66 per cent said so. At Whittier College, of 27 men students, 89 per cent said they wanted a boy and of 65 women students, 62 per cent said so. Since the male sex choice frequencies of Ohio State and Whittier College Students are essentially the same, we can show a combined table of their preferences for first and for only children.

Table 13

Percentage Distribution of Male Sex Preference for First and for Only Children as Reported by Two Student Groups at Ohio State and Whittier College Combined

	PREFERENCES EXPRESSED BY			
	Men Students		*Women Students*	
MALE SEX PREFERENCE FOR				
Hypothetical *first* child*	(145)	91%	(201)	86%
Hypothetical *only* child	(212)	91%	(260)	65%

* Difference between percentages in this row is not significant at the .05 level.

It is evident from table 13 that men's feelings of male sex preference is as strong in the case of a first child as in the case of an only child. Women, however, modify their overwhelming male preference considerably. Twenty-one per cent fewer women declare preference for a boy as an only child than as a first child. But in spite of this modification of their preponderant preference for a boy as an only child, two-thirds of the women students remain oriented toward a boy. For the college women we can therefore hardly speak of a natural predilection for girls.

However, these data for women college students should not be taken as representative of women in general. We know that women who look toward marriage typically defer to the outlook and interests of the men in their social circle, particularly to the marriageable ones. If we assume that women tend to be aware of, and sensitive toward, the cultural forces which make for male sex preference by men, we may confidently take it that women will defer their own less pressing values in the interest of more immediate goals such as engagement or marriage to a man in the group of which they are now members. In other words, it seems reasonable to suggest that in spite of our student data, women might prefer girls when their choice is unencumbered by dependence on men. To test this proposition we need data about women whose position in marriage is relatively secure and who, having already given birth to at least one child, are not role handicapped in terms of parenthood. Presumably such women would be less dependent on the outlook of their husbands and therefore less inclined to defer to the husbands' opinions and attitudes in matters of crucial importance to women. In other words, if there were a basic preference for girls among women, as was suggested in the hypothesis we are testing, this preference should become evident in such a group.

Fortunately for our purposes, such data happen to be available through the Indianapolis Studies of the Milbank Memorial Fund. Clare and Kiser (1951) have reported data for 1,309 fecund couples who were asked about their retrospective sex preference for a hypothetical only child: Table 14 reports this sex preference for husbands and wives who have had at least one child born to them. Once again we note men to be principally oriented toward boys. While being a parent of a girl child lowers the proportion of husbands wanting boys, we note that two-thirds of such fathers still prefer boys for only children. But with women the picture is quite different. Seventy-six per cent of the mothers who have had boys would again want a boy, if it had to be an only child; while of the mothers who have had girls, 84 per cent would want a girl if they could have only one child. These women are not as beholden to men's attitudes as were the women students. As we suspected, neither are they strongly attached to male preference. Limited information is also available about women who adopted a child by themselves. Gordon cites data on eight unmarried women who became adoptive mothers, one of these women being a divorcee. Of these eight, four adopted boys. Once again, one does not have the impression of an overwhelming drive for girl children on the part of women. But if women are not principally oriented toward girls, what is their orientation? Table 14 suggested that while men do indeed demonstrate a rather rigid male preference pattern, women are apparently oriented primarily toward the sex of the child they have already had. Women, in other words, are likely to think of the pleasures of motherhood

Table 14
Percentage Distribution of the Sex Preferences for Hypothetical Only Children as Retrospectively Reported by Fecund Husbands and Wives*

		HYPOTHETICAL SEX PREFERENCE AMONG COUPLES WHOSE FIRST CHILD WAS A			
		BOY		*GIRL*	
		Husband (N = 442)	*Wife (N = 306)*	*Husband (N = 313)*	*Wife† (N = 311)*
Retrospectively would want a	**Boy**	94%	76%	67%	16%
	Girl	6%	24%	33%	84%

* Table modified from Table I in Clare and Kiser (1951, 446).

† The discrepancy between the numbers of husbands and wives is due to the fact that those who had no preference were omitted from this table.

in terms of a specific child and would not want to alter that if given a new opportunity. We might think of it as a pragmatic child-centeredness of women once they are relatively free to express their own values, untrammelled by dependence on the outlook of men.

If the data from the student and the Indianapolis studies are a guide to women's true sex preference pattern, we must reject the explanation of their narcissistic concern with female preference in adoption. For leads to an understanding of the phenomenon of female sex preference we must look in a different direction.

AN ALTERNATIVE HYPOTHESIS

The core of a new hypothetical explanation of preference for girls in adoption was supplied by Brenner who suggested that such preference might arise from the couple's fear that the adopted child could not fully become a member of their family. On the basis of what we know about women's relative child-centeredness, we shall rephrase Brenner's idea in terms of men's fears. We shall hypothesize that: (a) Men are relatively hesitant in approaching adoption; (b) a hesitancy which is related to kinship sentiments. (c) With the wife as the most obviously deprived party, anxious for adoption, and the husband hesitant, a girl may represent a compromise solution for them.

With this hypothesis we have sought to locate the source of preference for girls in adoption among men, and have suggested that the ultimate cause must be looked for in sentiments which surround kinship. The several parts of the hypothesis will now be subjected to investigation.

Men are relatively hesitant in approaching adoption. In their study of Cornell student attitudes toward marriage and parenthood, Rockwood and Ford (1945) sought to discover under what circumstances the students would be willing to adopt a child. Table 15 demonstrates that men are consistently more reluctant to adopt than women are.

Table 15
Percentage Distribution of Cornell Men and Women Students by the Conditions Under Which They Would be Willing to Adopt a Child*

Would Adopt if	*Men (N = 190)*	*Women (N = 174)*
Could have none of own	84.7%	93.7%
Have one child but could have no more	44.7%	67.2%
Relative or close friend died, leaving child†	45.2%	57.0%

* Table modified from Rockwood and Ford (1945, 157).
† Difference between percentages in this row is not significant at the .05 level.

In spite of the fact that the figures in Table 15 show men to be more reluctant in their approach to adoption, the objection may quite properly be raised that this conclusion derives from the attitudes of students who are not yet involved in the realities of marriage and parenthood. The Eastern City study, however, provides us with information about the attitudes of householders, the majority of whom were married. From its data, we learn that the sentiments toward adoption expressed by men respondents are consistently more hesitant than those expressed by women.

The available evidence therefore tends to confirm the first part of our hypothesis which states that men are relatively hesitant in approaching adoption.

Men's hesitancy toward adoption is related to kinship sentiments. This second hypothesis will now be put to the test.

In Chapter 2 we had seen that by and large the adopters' parents approve of plans for the adoption of a first child. However, we also learned that husbands' fathers are more pronounced in their disapproval than wives' fathers. Also, approval of the adopters' parents was more easily forthcoming when the couple was childless than when they already had a child of their own.

Such findings suggest the survival of traditional values, most likely derived from a patrilineal kinship system in which male heirs are needed to carry on the family line. We shall now conceive of these traditional values and the kinship pattern which presumably promotes them as the source of male hesitancy in adoption. But if considerations of family line were involved in the phenomenon of differential sex preference, they should be more readily in evidence in the tradition-oriented family than in families where traditional values have little power. To put this idea to the test we should have an index of traditionalism among adopters, but such an index is not currently available. However, a substitute index may be had and for it we must once again turn to the work on male sex preference, reported by Dinitz, Dynes, and Clarke (1954).

These investigators raised the question whether a preference for boys by people who consider themselves fecund is traditional or affectional in origin. They concluded that, "Neither the aspirational level of the students nor the satisfaction of their affectional relationships with parents, siblings and peers of the same (or opposite) sex, contribute to the explanation of sex preferences" (1954, 129). Instead, their data point toward traditional group membership as responsible for male sex preference: Catholic and Jewish respondents showed a stronger male preference than did Protestants. This difference was significant at the .05 level. In addition, significantly fewer Protestants had a definite preference for the sex of the first child" (1954, 129). In seeking to explain these relationships, Dinitz and his coworkers argued as follows: ". . . the more cohesive the group memberships a person had, the greater the desire for a male child. In other words, those individuals who belonged to "traditional" groups—certain ethnic and religious groups—would exhibit a decided male preference" (1954, 128). Thus Catholics and Jews were regarded to be part of more traditional and cohesive family patterns than Protestants, and the latter were thought less committed to such patterns. In other words, these investigators used religious affiliation as an index of the sentiments which the kinship system tends to transmit to persons.

The relationship between religion and family attitudes is no mere conjecture. Dinkel (1944, 370-379) investigated the degree of commitment shown by high-school and college students to the value of supporting aged parents. He showed that Catholics more often than Protestants believed in this obligation.

Dinitz and his colleagues apply the index of religious affiliation to the explanation of male preference among college students. While these investigators sought to understand the sources of male preference in situations of assumed fecundity, we seek to understand the sources of female preference among nonfecund adopters. What now occurs to us is that the same forces, namely traditional kinship-based sentiments, make for male preference when fecundity is assumed *and* for female preference when nonfecundity is understood to be the couple's lot. Our argument for this contention runs along the following lines:

In the patrilineal societies of Hebraic, Greek, and Roman times, a male heir was considered a necessity for the continuation of the family line. The biblical institution of the levirate and the Greek and Roman practice of adoption arose out of, and helped affirm, the superior value of sons. In these societies, sons had social utility; they served certain real interests of the kin group, which explains the importance that was attached to sons. Such utility can hardly be ascribed to sons in the modern kin group, which reckons descent through the lines of father and mother and where sons seldom have a specific religious or economic function. But our observation suggests, and the work of Dinitz *et al.* confirms, that some groups seem to have a continued concern with a male heir, possibly as a symbol of family continuity.

If the husband in a childless union were to harbor such traditional sentiments concerning the importance of a male heir, adoption might very well pose a special threat to him. It would confirm and perpetually remind him of his inability to provide this symbol of family continuity. This may be his own feeling, or it may be supported by others in the wider kin group. Our suggestion then is that for tradition-oriented men, adoption poses a threat, because it breaks the continuity of the consanguine family. This threat should be considerably abated if a girl rather than a boy is being considered, since a girl will not carry the family name into subsequent generations.

These speculations can be tested, partially at least, by means of religious affiliation as an index of traditionalism. If traditional sentiments were at the source of female preference in adoption, we should expect Catholics and Jews, with presumably more traditional family sentiments than Protestants, to show a greater incidence of female preference than the latter. Data to test this proposition came from the 1960 study of agency records in which four agencies furnished anonymous information about the adopters who had originally been selected for the mail questionnaire study. Under the circumstances of application to an agency, one must expect spouses to present a common front, so that it is not surprising to find that husbands and wives almost invariably agreed on their sex preferences as set down in these records. When the sex preference information is examined by the religious group membership of the applicants, it is found that Catholics are indeed more prone to voice preference for girls than are Protestants. Of 557 Protestant husbands who stated a distinct sex preference at the time of application, 45 per cent said they wanted a girl. But of 108 Catholic husbands with a distinct preference, 54 per cent wanted a girl. No data for Jewish adopters were available from this agency source, but we do have Brenner's information of a decade earlier. Of the 50 couples whom she studied, 39 had originally voiced a preference. Twenty-eight, or 72 per cent, of these 39 had expressed a preference for a girl (Brenner, 1951, 35). This difference between the sex preference patterns of Catholics and Protestants was not quite significant at the .05 level. Knowing that sex preference also varies with age, older adopters being more inclined to ask for girls, it was decided to control the relationship between religious affiliation and sex preference on age. In other words, the relationship would be studied in different age groups. When that was done, it became evident that among male adopters of 38 years and over, Catholics no longer furnished a higher proportion of female sex preference. Once this age group was removed from the rest, a significant relationship resulted between religious affiliation and sex preference. Of 340 Protestant husbands between 22 and 38 years old, 37 per cent wanted girls; whereas of 75 Catholic husbands in that age group, 52 per cent had a preference for a girl.

We have thus obtained support for the view that tradition-oriented groups, here represented by Catholics, furnish a significantly greater proportion of preference for girls in adoption than do members of less tradition oriented groups, as represented by Protestants. We can now sum up our argument to say that *male hesitancy in adoption is apparently derived from affiliation with groups which uphold traditional kinship values.*

SOME MODIFYING FACTORS

Although we have reason to regard tradition-oriented group membership as the principal force making for female sex preference in adoption, we must recognize that there are also other influences which work for or against female sex preference. One of these, namely the age of the adopters was already mentioned.

Another modification seems theoretically likely as a result of economic forces. We recalled above that adoption in Greece and Rome was instrumental; it served the family line interests of patrician groups, especially with respect to the tenure of land holdings and political power. Why should current economic interests be less capable of encouraging men to enter adoption without female sex preference? Or, to put it differently, where the presence of sons is economically an asset we would expect to find less female sex preference than otherwise. On the family farm and in small business enterprises the presence of sons is frequently an asset. The data at our disposal are unfortunately not recent ones but are derived from the earlier decades of this century. Theis (1924, 221) reported information on children placed in foster care and adoption homes by the State Charities Aid Association of New York between 1898 and 1922. Of 1,612 foster and adoptive households whose locality characteristics were ascertainable, 757 were urban and 855 were rural. Of the children placed in urban households, 76.3 per cent were girls; while of the children placed in rural households, 53.7 per cent were girls. These figures suggest that the rural household, which was more likely to make good use of the services of a male child than an urban household could, was considerably more inclined toward boys than the latter.

Gordon (1930, 71) investigated a possible relationship between the adoptive parents' occupation and the sex of the child they took. She was concerned about the fact that the small number of cases on which her observations were based might make these observations spurious. But the recurrence of similar relationships between occupation and sex preference strengthens her case. Thus, the usual sex ratio among children adopted in Hamburg was one boy to two girls. But this relationship was conditional, depending on the socio-economic position of the adopters, as indicated by those cases for whom Gordon was able to obtain such information. Among 59 white collar workers, there were 16 (27 per cent) who adopted boys; and among 7 teachers there were 2 (30 per cent) who took boys. In contrast, among 18 owners of small businesses, there were ten (56 per cent) who took boys; and among 59 owners of larger businesses there were 23 (41 per cent) who adopted boys.

These data suggest that when occupational and economic interests favor the adoption of boys, as in farming or urban entrepreneurial activities, the tendency toward female sex preference recedes somewhat. We have thus indicated that at least three factors are instrumental in the appearance of female sex preference in adoption: values that are inculcated and sustained by particular reference groups, age, and socio-economic circumstances. Of these, we have come to regard the value factor as preceding or independent, and the other two as intervening or modifying.

The argument to date may be summarized as follows: (1) men tend to be relatively hesitant in approaching adoption, (2) this hesitancy derives principally from traditional values which have their source in certain group relationships.

DIFFERENTIAL SEX PREFERENCE AS AN ALIENATIVE RESPONSE TO ROLE HANDICAP

In trying to explain why differential sex preference occurs, we can now combine the idea of masculine hesitancy with the impact of traditional fecundity values by reference to the concept of role handicap. Until we came to this chapter, we had seen that the couple's role handicap principally affects the wife. She is apparently the more deprived, since her roles as childbearer and childrearer have been mutilated in childlessness and could only be partially restored in adoption. Her handicap is manifest. But now we have come upon this peculiar phenomenon of differential sex preference and the fact that men are more hesitant to adopt, especially when they adhere to traditional groups and the sentiments these foster. Do these factors not suggest that men, at least those with traditional family orientations, suffer a special deprivation in childlessness? We are here suggesting that they are indeed deprived, namely of the opportunity to provide consanguine members for the kin group. This, and the potential conflicts it poses with the marriage partner, makes the traditional man role handicapped in his own right. Where traditional kinship organization is capable of regulating indivdual behavior, this role handicap is likely to be institutionally recognized and provided for. Thus, Patai (1959, 121-122) considers barrenness to constitute the most frequent ground for divorce in the patriarchal kinship groups of the modern Middle

East. This institutional provision for combating childlessness is also reflected in ancient Jewish law. More directly, we have all witnessed the operation of this mechanism a few years ago when the present Shah of Iran divorced a wife whom he apparently loved but who was barren. Under such circumstances of dynasty or kinship-regulated behavior, the man is well aware of the nature of his handicap. But where the impact of kin organization has receded, as among the contemporary urban middle classes, the man's overt role handicap is bound to recede with it. As we saw in Chapter 2, values emphasizing fecundity have not disappeared. The data on preference for male children in social circumstances that require no special male attributes such as physical strength suggest the survival of nonfunctional values. It may be that these values make themselves felt especially when men find that their marriages are barren. With no kin group actively prodding them, there should be a latent role handicap for tradition-oriented men, manifesting itself in a sense of uneasiness. This latent role handicap makes such a man alienated from fecundity values that would ordinarily have predisposed him to desire a son. Thus alienated, he may wish to have no family, or, if for some reason he still wants children, he will most likely prefer a girl.

Let us see whether we can bring some facts to bear on this assertion. If differential sex preference is indeed an index of alienation, we should find that people with a choice for a girl would tend to make the adoptive situation into a different one than would those who are not so alienated, that is, those who either wanted a boy or had no sex choice. Specifically, we would expect the more alienated to feel more hesitant about expanding their adoptive family beyond the first child and to be oriented toward "rejection-of-difference." The relationship between the nonfecund couple's original sex preference and the eventual size of their adoptive family is as follows: Of 364 couples who at the time of their first application to an agency jointly said they had no sex preference, 35 per cent adopted only one child; of 335 such couples who had asked for a boy, 33 per cent remained one-child familes; but of 288 couples who had asked for a girl, 56 per cent adopted only one child. We see that people with an original preference for a girl are significantly more hesitant than are those with a preference for boys, or those without preference, to expand their adoptive family beyond one child.

We have another objective index of the couple's orientation toward the adoptive situation. The mail questionnaire of 1956 was clearly labeled "Adoption Research Project." In answering it, the respondents took a minimum step in the direction of acknowledging their position as adopters. While some of the questionnaires most likely did not reach the people to whom they were addressed, the bulk of nonresponses must be assumed to represent people who made the decision not to reply. It was therefore argued that response to the questionnaire should serve as an index of orientation toward the adoptive parental role. In this light, nonresponse was interpreted as a form of "rejection-of-difference." The relationship between the original sex preferences expressed at the time of application (checked in the 1960 study of agency records) and responses to the mail questionnaire is as follows: Of 344 nonfecund couples who, when first applying for a child, jointly claimed to have no sex preference, 59 per cent responded to the mail questionnaire. Of the 334 couples who had expressed a preference for a boy, 54 per cent replied to the questionnaire. (The difference between these percentages is not significant.) But of 274 couples who had originally asked for a girl, only 41 per cent responded. Here again we find significant differences between the original sex choice and the couple's readiness to acknowledge their adoptive position. Couples who had had no sex preference were the most likely to respond and couples who had stated a preference for a boy were significantly more prone to return their questionnaires than those who had asked for a girl.

But both the size-of-family and the response index could have varied with sex preference because of other factors which we know to influence the size of family and the readiness to respond to a request for a written report such as the questionnaire. Age, socio-economic status, and in the case of size-of-family, the length of time that elapsed between the first adoption and the receipt of the questionnaire, might readily account for the differences we have observed in the tables here shown. The relationship between sex preference and size-of-family on the one hand, and sex preference and response rate on the other, were therefore controlled on age, socio-economic status, and the period between the first adoption and the receipt of the questionnaire. In each instance, the relationship between sex preference and size-of-family, and sex preference and response rate remained essentially unaffected.

Given these facts, we can feel relatively certain that differential sex preference in the case of nonfecund adopters represents an alienative response to the role handicap suffered in childlessness. If we now return to the view that the husband is handicapped in his traditional role as representative of a patrilineal kin group, we should expect the choice for a girl to be essentially his. However, none of the data at our disposal directly show this; all we can point to is the tendency of the couple, at the time of application, to present a common front. Contrary to our view, we have Brenner's clinical observation: "Often the prospective father seems to feel that his wife suffers more by the childlessness, and that her normal narcissistic preference for a girl should be followed" (Brenner, 1951, 38).

Our view was expressed in the last part of our explanatory hypothesis and it will bear repeating here:

> *With the wife as the most obviously deprived party, anxious to adopt, and the husband hesitant, a girl may represent a compromise solution for them.*

While Brenner regards the woman as the source of preference for a girl, on the basis of the considerations brought together here, we suspect that the truth is quite otherwise. Rather than husbands concurring with wives in the wives' narcissistic preference for girls, we believe that wives are sensitive to their husbands' latent role handicap. By hinting to their husbands that they, the wives, would like a girl, they can allow the husbands to attribute their own feelings of alienation to their wives. Role handicapped husbands can therefore minimize their own role handicap and maximize the satisfactions they and their wives get from the companionship of a child. We have called this a "compromise," because by voicing a preference for a girl, wives enable their husbands to move toward adoption and thus assure themselves of the opportunity for motherhood.

CONCLUDING REMARKS

This has indeed been a speculative detour. The facts we have been able to marshal about differential sex preference suggest that this phenomenon reflects the sense of powerlessness of tradition-oriented husbands in nonfecund unions.

If our speculations are at all correct, we can infer that pioneering enterprises cannot remove contradictions of this order. Where tradition-oriented husbands are relatively hesitant to move toward adoption and where the adoption of a girl as a first child represents a compromise for the nonfecund couple, we can in part rely on the working of time to make such husbands more comfortable with their new substitute parental role. But not all needs to be left to time and to chance. Only in agency adoptions is there scope for sex preference. Rather than identify sex preference as a sign of the couple's ambivalence toward adoption, social workers may more appropriately help adoptive applicants by giving them an understanding of the working of traditional forces. Assuming that other factors are satisfactory and that the couple can be given a girl, the new father can now be helped to think ahead to a second child. This approach stresses the educative function of social work in adoption. Our next chapter will deal in detail with the implications of our theory of adoptive relations for social work.

CHAPTER NINE

*

And Set Their Minds to It

*

WHAT are the meanings and implications of this book for professional work in adoption and for the mental health professionals who serve members of adoptive familes? The ultimate assessment of the theory is properly the task of those who are engaged in practice in the field. But a few questions may facilitate such discussions.

In Chapter 1, the fertility expectations of married couples were compared with the actuality encountered by the nonfecund seeking compensation in adoption. We saw that adopters are typically deprived of a bio-social experience which they had grown up to regard as of major value. In Chapter 2 we saw that other people around the adopters also tend to reinforce the sense of loss and deprivation. Some of these enforcing sentiments stemmed from relatives and from the social work literature. But most impressive was the weight of public attitudes meeting adopters in casual questions and remarks by outsiders.

These sentiments emphasize the substitutive, second-best, nature of adoptive parenthood, and thereby serve to continue the adopters' role handicap. Nor can the indiscreet remarks of others be attributed simply to people who "don't know better," thus to the unfeeling, and to those with less formal education and sophistication than is usually found among adoptive parents and social workers. This was dramatically illustrated by an incident that occurred some months ago. A fellow social scientist had seen the mimeographed lectures on which part of this book is based. He and his wife were childless and happened at that time to have applied to an adoption agency to get a child. Both commented on the lectures saying that too much had been made of other people's attitudes: "We've never met up with anything like that—and if we did, it wouldn't bother us." Not long after this occasion, at a professional conference, this colleague confided the following occurrence. His wife had received a telephone call from an old school friend who had just had her first baby. In the course of the conversation, the childless woman mentioned that she and her husband were hoping to adopt a baby. The friend is recalled to have remarked: "You are fortunate that you can have yours without the problems of a pregnancy." How had his wife reacted? "Well," he said, "Mary seems to have gotten pretty mad and told her friend a thing or two!" However sophisticated we may believe ourselves to be, to the extent that we share with others certain cultural values, is the extent to which we are also vulnerable when our position with regard to these values is called into question. These views lead to several queries concerning practice:

> To what degree are child-placement workers currently aware of cultural forces which are likely to impinge on nonfecund couples entering on adoption?
>
> What part do social workers, directly and through their professional literature, play in structuring or in modifying some of the existing community sentiments?

> What do social workers currently contribute to a realistic orientation on the part of adopting couples toward the social and cultural forces that surround them?

Social workers are well aware that the situations of application, interviews, and waiting produce considerable stress for their clients. They also know that stressful situations are not conducive to an optimal presentation of self in related interpersonal transactions. We might then ask:

> Are such understandings made part of the assessment of an applicant's fitness for parenthood? Or, is due allowance made for the impact that the dependency in which the clients find themselves at the time of application may itself contribute to their sense of inadequacy and thus to a poor presentation of self?

In the course of the discussion of parental dilemmas, attention was drawn to the fact that the role-handicapping experiences of childlessness and of the preplacement period are subsequently carried over into adoptive family life. Some of the issues related to the dilemmas were clearly recognized by Brenner (1951), who indicated that adoptive parents lean in the direction of "rejection-of-difference" and that workers frequently sanction such an orientation by their own attitudes:

> Often workers said that parents would need to feel comfortable about discussing (birth and adoption) with their children before they could do it, *but there is no indication in the records that workers themselves had understood the full complexity of the problem for parents and child alike. . . .*
>
> (Workers) did not recognize fully the emotional problem inherent in the situation which might possibly become more acute as the family ties strengthened. It was difficult for workers to recognize how complicated and difficult a problem this necessarily is. There is a tendency to over-simplify the complexity of the adoptive relationship. *Workers tend to be happier if they can think of it as exactly like the usual parent-child relationship and without special problems in a home where families really love and accept children* 1951, 72-73 (Emphases added.)

On the basis of these observations, we may now inquire:

> To what extent have these findings been understood and in what ways have they been incorporated into professional practice?

There are indications that some workers continue to view the adoptive situation in much the same way as described by Brenner. Thunen (1958) has reported an agency innovation in work with adoptive clients. Toward the end of the period of supervision of their home, the parents are invited to the agency for a kind of "graduation" party, a rite of passage into full-fledged adoptive parenthood. During such meetings the adopting couples share with each other and with the workers present some of their parental experiences of the previous months:

> Sometimes parents who have a natural child will tell us of their beginning feelings toward that child, as compared with the feeling of parenthood toward an adopted child. From such parents the group will hear at first hand that *there is no essential difference in the long run between parenthood by adoption and parenthood by the biological process* (1958, 11). (Emphasis added.)

The author apparently approves of this point of view, for in the preceding passage she says:

> *As to their feeling about infertility, which was discussed so much in the adoption study, they rarely think about that now.* When they do, it is sometimes with a sense of shock. If they had had a child by biological process, it wouldn't have been Jimmie! Unique individual that he is, he had become their very own. *When they begin to talk like this it is about time for them to go to court* (1958, 10). (Emphases added.)

This seems to indicate that the author sanctions the adoptive parents' desire to slough off their self-image as atypical parents, to move from "acknowledgment-of-difference" to "rejection-of-difference." Perhaps this is an issue that goes deeper than the desires and feelings of individual workers. Perhaps we should look carefully at the prescriptions which have been formulated for adoptive relations.

The first of these prescriptions bids the would-be parents to "accept" their nonfecundity, to come to grips emotionally with the fact that they could not have offspring of their own. The second prescription bids them to tell their child of the adoption and to do so early in the child's life. You might say: "Of course, these are prescriptions for your 'acknowledgment-of-difference' pattern. The first prescription makes the parents acknowledge the difference of their situation, and the second prescription makes it a consistent acknowledgment with the child. Professional analysis has quite correctly assessed the adoptive situation and has based its practice prescriptions properly on that assessment." I would be tempted to reply: "Hold on a moment —you are quite right in thinking that each of the prescriptions is valid in itself; each is certainly in line with what we have found in our research. Nevertheless I have some doubts concerning the prescriptions."

But, if nothing is wrong with either prescription individually, what else might possibly be unsatisfactory? It is their lack of coordination. It is as if a physician had seen the necessity of two drugs for his patient's illness and had prescribed them to be administered without consideration of the effect these two drugs in combination have on the patient. Similarly, it seems that the prescriptions for adoptive relations have been developed apart from each other.

The effect of this lack of coordination is demonstrated in services which remain unused even though clients may be in need of them:

> Many workers suggested that if [telling the child] presented a problem later, the families could return to the agency for help with it.
>
> In practice, although some of the families indicated in the current study some difficulty and conflict over how to handle the telling of adoption to the child, it had not occurred to any of them to return to the agency for such a service. By this time the children are well assimilated into their family life, and the adoption agency which originally gave them the child seems quite remote to them. *Families who have difficulty with this,* perhaps

> even more than some of the others, *would like to forget this is an adopted child and the agency was its source* (Brenner, 1951, 73). (Emphases added.)

Since Brenner's observations were made there have evidently been changes in the way some agencies define their place relative to the needs of adoptive parents and children. The following quotations make clear one agency's changed orientation and the effects that this seems to have had on the readiness of adoptive parents and children to ask for help. It is especially interesting to note that these changes are reported for the very agency whose cases Brenner studied.

> For the agency to think of legal adoption as a barrier between it and the adoptive family, and to allow them to think of it that way, is to deny that there are special features in the needs of adopted children and to make it more difficult for the family to meet these needs. Our recognition that adoptive parents face special problems is consistent with our symbolizing the differentness of adoptive parenthood, and *our affirmative offer of help after legal adoption should serve not to threaten their feelings of adequacy but to lessen their need for denial* (Sandgrund, 1962, 249). (Emphasis added.)

> Parents or grown adopted children often have taken the initiative in asking for help. We have found that generally adoptive parents return in later years because of concern about the handling of adoption, or because of a physical or developmental problem in the child (Brown, 1959, 21-22).

Nevertheless, although Sandgrund recognizes that "the affirmative offer of help . . . should serve to lessen their need for denial," this is not the same as instructing clients in the coordinated use of the two prescriptions. It seems that this step has yet to be evolved clinically, and we should now study the question:

> How can social work in adoption best coordinate its prescriptions for its clients? What steps can it take to assure consistency in "acknowledgement-of-difference" by clients for their children and for themselves?

The question of patterns of client coping also affects the larger field of agency services. How do clients use the services offered? Do they ever, wittingly or unwittingly, misuse them? If it were found that the organization of adoption services, intended for one objective, latently came to serve another, it would presumably be of concern to the agency. In that light, let us look at a number of coping patterns that we have met before and that were previously regarded as of the "rejection-of-difference" type. Against these, let us place aspects of the agency's service that might be considered to reinforce such orientations on the part of the client.

Parental Coping Patterns of the Type of "Rejection-of-Difference" in Relation to Agency Practice

Client Coping Patterns	*Professional Practices*
"Forgetting" the Adoption.	The agency "leaves the scene" after legalization of the adoption.
Myth of Family's Origin (adopters as principal focus: "The child was *meant* for us").	The agency initiates the prescription for "telling the child," but it does not offer the parents means for dealing with the resulting dilemma of Integration vs. Differentiation.
Myth of Family's Origin (child as principal focus: The parents looked for the right child and chose him).	Social work literature and agency personnel are frequently responsible for the adopters' use of the "chosen child" approach.
Minimizing the Impact of "Telling."	Some agencies give the adopters a general background story, or tell only such parts of the child's background which the adopters are thought ready to accept. Confidentiality of agency and court records insures adopters against chance discovery, by the child, of matters not revealed by the parents.
Avoiding the Image of the Natural Parents.	The agency's role as mediator obviates direct dealings between natural and adoptive parents. Also, agencies generally seek to place children in homes at some geographical distance from the residence of the natural parents (Schapiro, 1956; I, 84).

Parental Coping Patterns of the Type of "Rejection-of-Difference" in Relation to Agency Practice (*Continued*)

Client Coping Patterns	*Professional Practices*
Simulation of the Biological Family's Physical Appearance.	It is common practice for agencies to try matching the appearance of the adoptive parents and the child, or, less commonly, the matching of the appearances of people in the child's ancestry to the appearances in the adoptive family (Schapiro, 1956; 1, 84).
Simulation of the Biological Family's Spacing of Arrival of Children.	It appears to be the common practice of child-placing agencies to insist that a "suitable" period elapse before an application for an additional child can be accepted.
Simulation of the Biological Family's Constellation of the Ages of Children Relative to Their Arrival in the Family.	Agencies are apparently reluctant to place a second or subsequent child who is older than the child who preceded him into the family.
Infancy Adoption (simulation of the biological family's appearance through adoption of very young infant).	Professional practice has relatively recently put increasing emphasis on placement in the early weeks of life. This orientation was stimulated by the publication of the Bowlby (1951) Report.
Fending off Inquiries from Outsiders.	Confidentiality of agency and court records insures the adopters against the intrusion by outsiders into their family secrets.
Symbols of Changed Identity.	Current practice supports the issuance of new birth certificates at the time of legal adoption. These certificates show the child's new name and avoid reference to a former family status.

Our critic is likely to ask: "Are you suggesting that these agency patterns should be changed because they happen to coincide with the tendency of clients to use them for 'rejection-of-difference'?" The answer is "No." Nor is it to be suggested that each one of the client patterns is in itself undesirable; after all, it is desirable that a child, whose adoption is necessary, be adopted as early in life as possible. The problem with infancy adoption enters, from our point of view, when the adopter uses it to "forget that this was an adopted child," to move with it toward "rejection-of-difference." What we wished to do here was to point to the fact that adoptive clients may seek to utilize a variety of legitimate, and frequently necessary, professional instruments for purposes which may ultimately defeat their own and the profession's goals for them. This observation leads us to ask:

> How can the pattern of agency services be made to take into account the tendency on the part of clients to use these services in self-defeating ways?

Adoptive parents must be able to think about and have empathy with the natural parents in order that they can most effectively help the child in his questioning about his background. We should then consider:

> Are there ways in which adoptive parents can be helped to orient themselves empathically toward the natural parents? Might agencies explore the possibility of a meeting between the natural mother and the adopting parents before the child is placed with them? Such a meeting, carefully arranged and protected, could serve as an anchor for the adopters in their thoughts and feelings about their child's first parents. Also, might agencies, whenever possible, encourage the natural mother to write a letter that expresses her feelings toward the child and her motives for letting him be adopted? Such a letter might serve as a tie between the natural and the adoptive parents, and help the latter give their child information and support when these are needed. Finally, might adopters be encouraged to send to the agency a brief annual report on their child? The natural mother could thereby be given unidentifiable information if she inquired, and could thus be treated as a human being whose relinquishment of her child has not necessarily wiped out her feelings for him.[3]

Social workers know that the requirements and opportunities

3. For insights into the needs of some natural mothers and adopted persons I am indebted to the writings of Jean Paton.

of parenthood change with the changing situation of the family cycle.

> Can this fact be utilized in the education of adoptive parents for their roles? For instance, if it is known that adoptive parents now will most likely seek to adopt at least two children, would not the time of their application for a second child offer special opportunities for intensive work on the expanding requirements of the adoptive parent-child relationship?

Most of these questions have had a common theme. Social work in adoption as well as other mental health services for adoptive families has in large measure an educative function. The summary question is therefore:

> Seeing that adoptive parents have unique tasks to perform, for which there is little explicit guidance in the cultural script, what can professionals do toward setting the parents' minds effectively toward these tasks?

In this chapter we have considered some implications of our theory for the helping professions, particularly for social work. But in the end, the fate of the adoptive relationship is in the hands of its participants. We have as yet to ask how our theory can be made to work within the family, especially in the light of the child's growth and development.

CHAPTER TEN

*

Shared Fate

*

A COUPLE who patently understood an issue central to the adoptive relationship put these thoughts into their mail questionnaire reply: "We have missed a reference as to how parents are approaching the problem of the natural acceptance by the child of his unique position in the family and society. This may not be of apparent importance at first but will, no doubt, be the one single factor which will determine the future relationship between the child and his or her parents and society in general." In this final chapter let us take this formulation and ask ourselves what parents can do to help their child accept his position with comfort. The pioneering steps we have begun to outline in Chapter 7 are part of the answer, but now we want to show in detail how they can be brought into being. A number of parents have reported their approaches; these are now to be identified.

THE IDEOLOGICAL APPROACH

One adoptive mother writes that she and her family rely on the doctrine of human equality:

> We teach our children, in all areas of life, the doctrine of the equality of men. Every man, son of a king or son of backwoods incest, has the same intrinsic value. His potential value depends upon how well he uses his native abilities in contributing to society. By this and this alone is a man to be judged.
>
> This concept is very teachable, for it is, of course, the justification of political democracy; it is written into the Declaration of Independence; it is the basis for English common law and American jurisprudence; it is the cornerstone of the Judao-Christian ethic. A parent has a million ways to teach it, without relation to adoption at all: your attitude toward racial or religious prejudice; your reaction when someone says that so-and-so is "from a good family"; your respective response toward, say, Rita Hayworth and your cleaning woman. . . . It does not take long for a child to have engrained into the deepest consciousness the conviction that a man's value consists solely and entirely of what *he* is.

As part of the family's regular style of life this approach should go a long way toward the child's comfortable acceptance of himself. But by itself, ideological instruction does little to emphasize interdependence of the members of the family unit. We shall therefore accept the ideology of equality as pertinent, but as insufficient for the purpose of integrating the adopted child into his family.

THE APPROACH OF MUTUALISM OR "SHARED FATE"

Sentiments of belongingness are strengthened when members are engaged in mutual aid arising from mutual needs. The condition of mutual needs in the adoptive parent-child relationship is the condition of mutual need of all parent-child relations, enlarged and emphasized by the discrepancies and losses both parents and children have suffered. As a method of integrating the child into the family mutualism always begins with the parents. They must institute it and make it work. It is for them to set up the channels within which they can identify themselves with the child's situation, so that he, in his turn, can reach out to them and recognize them as the people to whom he unqualifiedly belongs. To be able to do this, the parents must have come to accept naturally, with comfort, *their* position in family and society.

As their child grows, he has to incorporate into his understanding an increasing number of complex concepts. Among these is the concept of adoption. Inevitably the question of why he was given up, and the problematic issues behind it, will press in on the child. He will therefore feel the need to make inquiries and where should he turn more naturally with these than to his parents? They, for their part, must be "on call," but that is a requirement that is easier formulated than carried out. How can they be "on call" when the requests for their attention come neither at specified times nor in predictable form? This is where our previous interest in empathy enters. The parents must somehow be able to sense when the child's activities are really requests for information and support. But too little is known about empathy and the way it works to give precise instructions for its implementation. However, we have some reports from adoptive parents who have apparently been able to achieve a degree of empathy satisfactory to them. The following ideas have been derived from a number of such reports.

It appears that empathic sensitivity has been attained through the recall of pain which the parents suffered in childlessness. This suggestion will at first glance appear to contradict the evidence presented in Chapter 5. There we saw that the greater the degree of the original deprivation, the greater also the reliance on modes of coping by "rejection-of-difference." Empathy was associated with "acknowledgment-of-difference." How then could the pain of deprivation be made to serve the expansion of empathic sensitivity? What the proponents of the method of the recall of pain seem to suggest is this: If the parents have undergone a re-evaluation of their experience, if they have faced squarely the ideas, sentiments, and feelings that were part of their frustrated expectations, they can in time remake the picture of themselves. The pain which once deeply involved the parent can now be recalled. In its new state it will be decontaminated, shorn of its nagging quality. Instead, it has become a source of strength, of greater self-awareness, and of increased awareness of others. In that way, recall of one's pain previously suffered can become a vehicle for apprehending the pain in others and their needs for help. Once self-defeating, the pain has become the raw material for the apparatus needed by the adoptive parents who wish to be "on call" for their child.

How is it possible to "work through" feelings of loss and defeat to the point where they lose their hold, where they no longer undermine one's sense of worth? In most circumstances this will require a certain amount of aid. Parents who have adopted through agency channels know that this is one of the objectives of social casework. But there are many others who have not had the same opportunity. They can, if they wish, avail themselves of the counseling services offered by family service agencies and mental health clinics, as well as by private psychological and psychiatric practitioners. Some of the adoptive parent associations, especially those whose membership is drawn largely from nonagency adopters, might want to investigate the provision of such professional services for their members. Pioneering frequently requires technical assistance as well as mutual aid.

THE CHILD'S NEEDS

The question will quite properly be raised whether we are not making more of the child's difficulties than he really has to face. All growing up, after all, poses problems. It is quite true that the concentrated manner of this discussion can leave a false impression. Much of the time the child will be unmoved by the issue of adoption. Only occasionally does he ask for aid, and at first in rather inarticulate ways. Here lies one of our major difficulties. Is it not likely that with our senses cocked sharply to the child's possible needs we will misunderstand the signals and find problems where in fact there are none? Such objections are valid. But we must also recall that where the cultural script is inadequate, the tune has to be played by ear; the artists have to improvise and that implies taking risks. Our question has to be whether the best calculated risk is in the direction of too little or too much sensitivity to the child's activities. If these activities have been misinterpreted, the matter can be dropped quickly enough. Presumably parents are capable of learning. By and by they should learn the evolving style of their child's way of asking, so that there will ultimately be less need for trial and error on their part. But if the child calls repeatedly and is not heard, he will become less and less inclined to express his feelings and the illusion will be created of a happy child who has none of these needs.

There can be little doubt that the child whom the parents have told of his adoption needs an expanding understanding of its meaning. But as he learns that the adoption became possible because another mother (and father) gave him up, he is likely to feel that the social ground under him is not firm. He therefore has a special need for experiences that will confirm for him his belongingness in the adoptive family. The need for such integrative experiences was poignantly illustrated by the boy whose remark was quoted in the Introduction: "The child who is born into his family is like a board that's nailed down from the start. But the adopted child, him the parents have to nail down, otherwise he is like a loose board in mid-air."

On the face of it, this process of "nailing the child down" would seem to require little more than parental affection. But if we think the matter through we will find that love is not enough. Being as yet "ego-centric" in the sense that he sees all social situations from the point of view of his own experiences, he will most likely regard the love he is experiencing as an essential ingredient of all parenthood. He also senses that the adoptive parents would not be able to part with him of their own free will. How is he then to understand that he was once given up by another mother and father? Moreover, his difficulty is compounded when the adults try to explain the fact of relinquishment as motivated by love. "Your first mother loved you so much that she wanted you to have a family of your very own when she could not make a home for you." Such a statement is reasonable to the adult mind only because we know and understand the power of impersonal social forces and how merciless these can be. Without any knowledge of such forces, the explanation of relinquishment based on maternal love will be confounding. For the child to be able to comprehend at all how love could have motivated his first mother to give him up, he requires some additional information. Without it, he might come to fear that, being loved in his present home, he might again be given up, imagining the death of one of his adoptive parents and with the widowed parent finding it difficult to make a home for him, he would out of love, again be given up. The child therefore needs certain bare facts to understand his situation. Logically, the facts of birth out of wedlock and its attendant social and psychological problems should help to explain the necessity and desirability of adoption. But this is the very explanation which, if applicable, many parents fear to give.

Our critic is likely to counter: "But logic is not all that matters here; the child will accept what we tell him in part because of the conviction which he gathers from our manner and tone of voice. If we personally can be comfortable with the information we give him, he too will feel comfortable with it." There is of course considerable truth in this. We will more likely influence our listener if we are convinced of what we are saying than if we are not. Even logically contradictory information is often accepted if presented with conviction. But the contradiction may presently become evident to the other party after all. Whether and how soon this happens depends on a number of circumstances. How intelligent is the subject? How important is the information for him; will he ponder it from time to time or will he let it go by? The information about relinquishment is patently important for the child; for on it hinges his understanding of why he was adopted. He is likely to be of at least average intelligence. His parents are not always with him to reinforce his acceptance of their statement, nor are they themselves likely to bring the matter up. This is why it seems likely that the adopted child, even after he has apparently accepted the explanation of his relinquishment as based on parental love, will after some time find himself again in a quandary to understand it. But since he is also likely to regard his parents as unimpeachable sources of information, he may begin to put his puzzlement down to his own inadequacy and unworthiness. He may even come to regard his own thoughts as evil and alien from theirs.

If this chain of reasoning has correctly assessed the situation in which the adopted child finds himself, then we will necessarily be led to a rather disconcerting conclusion. We must then conclude that the adopted child whom the parents have told that he was adopted will almost inevitably experience uncertainties about his belongingness as well as confusion about his identity. That is why he probably has especially urgent needs for open channels of communication with his parents, why he needs to be allowed to define freely the extent of his quest, and why he must have experiences which will confirm his membership in the adoptive family.

A METHOD FOR MEETING THE CHILD'S NEEDS

It has already been suggested that the parents' recall of their own deprivation and pain, worked through but not discarded, may provide an instrument for keeping open the channels of communication. Through such means they may be able to apprehend the occasions when the child seeks information and support. Now we shall make an additional suggestion. The method of the recall of pain may also enable the parents to throw in their lot with the child's and thereby let him experience the reality of his membership in the adoptive family. Two incidents will serve to demonstrate this dual function of the method.

The first incident concerns a child who had been in her adoptive home since early infancy. At the time she was not quite five years old. She was bright and had already asked several searching questions about adoption, which the mother had answered. A short while before the incident, the child started to wet her bed and to have nightmares. A visiting relative had previously brought her a book with the story of Cinderella, colorfully illustrated. The little girl had apparently fastened on that story. The parents did not like it; they seem to have sensed that it undermined their own substitute parental position. But the more the mother hesitated to read the book, the more the child insisted on it. Finally she demanded to have it read at bedtime, evening after evening. The adoptive mother began to suspect a connection between the child's insistence on the Cinderella story and the nightmares and bedwetting. But before she could do something about it the child made the overture herself. She said casually, "Mommy, if I had a stepmother, what would she do to me, would she be cruel?" The mother recognized the intent and importance of the question and replied: "My dear, I too am someone like a stepmother. I was unable to bear you in my body, but I love you very, very much. Perhaps there are stepmothers who are bad, who would be mean to their children. Cinderella's stepmother *was* a very bad mother, but only because she did not love Cinderella." There was a pause; the child seemed occupied with her toys. After some time she remarked: "Now I can have a good dream." And so it happened. The bedwetting and nightmares ceased abruptly.

This account strongly suggests that the adoptive mother was able to recall her own pain of deprivation and so to fit herself partially to the model of a stepmother, whose image in the story was the cue by which she understood the child's need. She was able to make an explanation which freed her child of feelings of confusion and inadequacy.

It is obvious from such an account that empathic communication must involve trial and error. Some attempts at understanding are bound to misfire and fail. Reports of failures would be as appropriate as reports of successes. If no failures are recorded here it is only because they have not been reported. The trial and error method may seem too risky to some parents. But when specific directives are unavailable, pioneering is called for, and pioneering involves taking risks. A case is on record which shows both the parental hesitation to take a risk and the way in which the shared fate approach was successfully brought into play when the risk was accepted.

A ten-year-old boy had been asking repeatedly about his original mother's identity. He specifically asked about her name. The adopting parents, feeling his mounting insistence, decided to tell him. On being questioned again the adoptive mother revealed the first mother's name. The son said: "When I am older, I'll change my name to hers." In subsequent conversation, the subject came up again. It was brought up by the boy in a manner that suggested that he wanted to challenge or test his father. The father made a reply of this order: "I think I understand a little of the way you feel. A name is a very personal possession. The name you had before you came to us was taken from you without you having any say in the matter. But a name is also a way of saying where we belong. So, if you should decide to change your name when you are grown up, and if I'm alive then, I will add your new name to our family name so that all of us can continue to belong together." During the following weeks there was a discernible shift in the boy's attitude. He had been inattentive at school and irritable at home.

Now he seemed to be less tense and he began to address himself with interest to his school work. Two months or more after the incident the father said to the boy half in jest: "You know what—I'm getting all ready to change my name," to which his son replied with a grin, "That won't be necessary now."

These incidents seem to reflect the potential utilty of the willingness to "acknowledge difference" and experience recall of pain. The method evidently enabled these parents to sense what their children's questions and behavior meant, and to use the occasion of giving the required information for throwing in their lot with the child's. In each case the consequence of the parental act was dramatically demonstrated by the child's statement and by the change in behavior. These changes leave little doubt that after the incidents the child felt himself on firmer social and psychic ground.

We have now dealt at some length with the idea of "shared fate," with the child's needs, and with a method which may aid the parents in meeting these needs. Now we must address ourselves to the question of how these needs appear in the course of the child's growth and development.

EARLY CHILDHOOD

With the rapid development of speech, the young child acquires his first notions of social roles, principally, of course, those roles which appear in the family drama. He comes to learn the meaning of different positions in the group and the regulations that govern them. But he has his own interpretations, autistic understanding, of these positions and regulations. Most likely his own adoption also will fall under the sway of autistic interpretation. Such was certainly the case when an adopted boy of five, while at supper with his parents, said as if out of the blue, "You stole me." Although apparently somewhat taken aback, the parents proceeded to correct his misconception of them and of the situation. In another case the child's autistic behavior made communication with the parent difficult. The mother overheard her five year old daughter saying to her doll: "When I'm grown up I'll be a *good* mother!" At first the adoptive mother assumed that the remark had been meant for her, but then she reflected that there had been no recent occasion for scolding or punishment. It occurred to her that the child was actually thinking about the natural mother. She questioned her daughter and found that her hunch had been correct. This mother was able to set her little girl's mind at ease about the natural mother. She explained that giving her up had been a very sad and hard experience but had been necessary under very difficult circumstances. Thereby she showed that the child's mother had in fact been a good mother, largely concerned with the little girl's well-being. By allowing the child to speak about the natural mother, the latter was included in the family situation. By explaining that she had *not* been a bad mother at all, a serious misunderstanding of her had been avoided. Klein covers such processes of communication in groups generally:

> The possibility of misunderstandings between members of the group is a constant danger. Great care must therefore be exercised not to hinder the opportunities for correcting the impression gained of other members of the group. If members of the group behave autistically and cut themselves off from communication with others, mistaken impressions will persist and morale in the group will be low (1956, 96).

MIDDLE CHILDHOOD

Wondering about origins may come earlier or later, but will almost certainly occur during the ages between six and twelve. A seven-year-old girl, learning that she was adopted at age one and a half remarked: "So no one wanted me before that." A seven-year-old boy: "If you hadn't told me, I wouldn't have to think about it now." An eight-year-old boy: "Do I have ancestors?" An eight-year-old girl: "If I ever met my first parents, would I know who they are?" A ten-year-old girl: "Do you mind if I sometimes think about my first mother?" A ten-year-old boy had been asking questions of his parents at bedtime. He had been speaking of his fantasies, saying that he sometimes had the feeling that his present life was a dream, that there existed another Johnny, the real one, and that the real Johnny was asleep when he was awake, and vice versa. The mother asked him whether he had the feeling that his present life and his parents were unreal. Johnny said, "Sometimes I feel that way, then I seem to forget all my experiences in our family and think that I really belong to another family."

Conklin (1920, 67) has shown that it is not uncommon for children to imagine that they were adopted. He showed that this fantasy occurred among his subjects most typically at ages eight through twelve for girls and ten for boys. For the child in his natural family this fantasy is a playful escape to be switched on and off as he has need for it; but for the adopted child it is a means toward understanding what for him is a reality. To a story like Johnny's or a remark "so no one wanted me before that," there is no easy answer. One thing is clear: Having once told the child that he is adopted, the adoptive parents who really practice "acknowledgment-of-difference" must share the child's thoughts of the natural parents. But the child is likely to sense how the parent feels about them: Do they pose a threat? Probably more is required than overt readiness to listen to the child and to answer questions factually. The parents' empathic capacity must also be able to envelop the child's forebears. We recall here the words of one empathic adoptive mother: "I felt a little uneasy about the natural mother parting with such a lovable baby and worried that she might be unhappy." In a study of such attitudes on the part of adoptive parents it was found that adopters who were relatively empathic toward the child (having recently wondered what their words about adoption might mean to the child) were also relatively empathic toward the natural parent (having recently wondered whether the biological mother ever thinks about the child).

The years of middle childhood, between six and twelve, see a wide expansion in the child's conceptual horizon. During this period, he is most likely ready to take in much of what he really needs to know for an understanding of his situation. It is the time when school and peer influences tend to replace those of the family. His conscience expands to include the idea of society and its rules. He learns that rules are made by men and that when men break the rules of society, painful consequences often result. He also comes to appreciate individual differences, that people are not all equally endowed and that some are more fortunate than others. All these conceptual learnings provide the ground on which his understanding of public aversion to illegitimate birth can be built. Although adoptive parents may find it difficult and unpalatable to give the child such information, this seems the appropriate time for him to learn the cultural meaning of out-of-wedlock birth from them. At this stage, the child is less personally vulnerable than he will be as an adolescent to the moral implications of the strictures related to sexual and reproductive norms. He should be able to absorb such ideas without feeling himself devalued. At the same time, the knowledge which he gains thereby will, more than any other, enable him to understand both the necessity and the desirabilty of his adoption. A girl of nearly nine was talking with her adoptive mother about the fact that she had been born to unmarried parents. She asked her mother: "If I ever had a baby that way, what would you do?" Her mother answered: "Of course I'd stand by you and would help you in any way I could, and so would Daddy. But that wouldn't solve the problem of the baby's future. That problem could not be easily solved. You would most likely have much suffering in finding the right thing to do for the baby and for yourself."

The preadolescent child typically spends much of his waking day among his age mates in the school and in the neighborhood. In that setting, he is not readily protected by parents and their explanations. The adopted child therefore needs a sense of competence about his adoption which can come only from his feeling that he has proper knowledge and that he can dispense it as he sees fit. The following questions and answers are from a ten-year-old's recollections:

"Is Sid your real brother?"
"Well, he is now, but before I was adopted he was not my brother. He wasn't with my other mother."

"Did you know your mother?"
"No, because I was adopted when I was a small girl."

"Were you in an orphanage?"
"I was in an agency. (When they ask what that means I go into a whole lot of stuff.)"

"Do you like this mother or the one you had before?"
"I didn't know the other mother but the one I have now is real nice."

"Why were you adopted?"
"That one I just skip."

ADOLESCENCE AND YOUNG ADULTHOOD

Teen-age persons frequently are uncertain about themselves, partly because of conflicting expectations held by parents, the peer group, and the school. This is a time when the intimate contact with parents is sloughed off and heterosexual peer relations are of paramount importance. If the adoptive parents have previously avoided giving the child satisfying information about his forebears, particularly with respect to illegitimacy, the child is likely to imagine the worst. Such a teen-age adoptee is thus likely to have especially serious self-doubts, feeling himself alienated from his parental moorings. A fifteen-year-old high-school girl reports that she has good relations with her adoptive parents ("we do a lot of things together"), but she worries about the fact that she was born out of wedlock. "I'm shy about boys and sex. I like boys, but when I get to know one I get scared." She is well aware of the fact that sexual attitudes are not inheritable, but having this background worries her nevertheless. There seems to have been only a minimum of communication on this matter with her parents.

A nineteen-year-old girl writes:

> I believe many parents underestimate the intelligence and curiosity of the seven- or eight-year-old child who can not get reasonable, concrete replies to his questions. There are always "ways" of finding more out about adoption, if the child is curious enough.
>
> There is also the desire to hear and know a little about the biological mother. From his adoptive home the child can gain everything and perhaps more than he could have from the biological family, but I think there is the innate desire in most everyone (adopted) *to stabilize himself with a little knowledge of his origin*—whether his mother and father were both blonds, or if one was Roumanian and one Scotch-Irish or what. *Thus, when the eternal growing up question of "Who am I?" presents itself, one will not feel so cheated as to a jumping off place for his thoughts.* (Emphases added.)

Remarks by other adopted persons carry much the same message: "To say that I have not thought about them would be ridiculous. Everyone at some time or another must wonder about ancestors." "No matter how civilized one is—the thoughts of heredity and marrying go hand in hand."

We have now looked at the way the child's needs appear in the course of his development. In early childhood, his tendency toward autistic thinking is likely to make him misunderstand his situation. For his own sake and that of the parent-child relationship, these misunderstandings should be cleared up when they become evident to the adults. Recurrent wondering about origins will most likely take place in middle childhood. Since that period seems also the one in which the child can most readily absorb information about the cultural meaning of out-of-wedlock birth, the middle years between seven and twelve present the parent with the optimum time for clarification of the meaning of adoption. Middle childhood then would appear crucial for establishing that "jumping off place" for thoughts about his identity, which mark the person in his teens.

SOCIAL AND PSYCHIC GROUND THROUGH ROLE COMPANIONS AND FAMILY RITUALS

Much of our emphasis in this chapter has been on parental awareness. Understandably the reader may have become impatient with this theme, knowing that people just do not keep up such efforts for long. Besides, he may regard a high level of awareness and rationality to conflict with the nature of family relations. Like relations in other primary groups, familial relations tend to be governed by sentiment and habit rather than by rationality and design.

Habits and sentiments are created and reinforced by regular and frequent interaction in a group. We should therefore expect that the sentiments created among adopted siblings are capable of supplying the adopted child with some of the social and psychic ground which he needs. As one adopted child with two adopted siblings has put it, "If I didn't have them, I'd feel so different." Such role companionship requires little awareness for its successful operation.

Family groups need times when awareness is allowed to lag and actions are carried out automatically. This is accomplished by rituals. In ritual activties, behavior is prescribed and routinized. Christmas and birthday celebrations have characteristics of routine which, while well known to the participants, are eagerly anticipated. Such routinized festivals bring members of the group together, give them each tasks toward the completion of common goals, and reinforce their sense of interdependence. This is what the celebration of the adoption anniversary, apparently so little resorted to, might do. The family party, perhaps with homemade song, could draw attention to the deeply satisfying aspects of shared fate.

However valuable annual observances may be, the simple rituals of everyday relationships can be equally significant—if not more so. In many families with school-age children, the main meal of the day represents the one time when all the actors are together, sporting, clashing, joking, making contact. Such rituals are capable of nourishing their "consciousness of kind."

But we are addressing ourselves in this chapter principally to the child's need for exploration of, and coming to grips with, his special position in family and society. There are rituals serving that need by supplying both child and parent with special opportunities for communication about the meanings of their situation. Keeping the family album up-to-date with pictures of the child's first days in the adoptive family, as well as of subsequent events, can be the stimulus for explorations around his evolving questions of identity. Some families have developed books in which special events are recorded alongside of snapshots. An adoptive mother has prepared the format of such a record book for use by adoptive parents and children. Although the title *All About You—An Adopted Child's Memory Book* (MacLeod, 1959) is somewhat inaccurate, since the book makes no mention of, or provison for, the child's preadoption history, it nevertheless may be a useful tool. In the hands of parents who are oriented toward "acknowledgment-of-difference," such a book may help the child to formulate further inquiries about himself and his origins.

Finally there is the simplest of all family rituals, the bedtime visit. What small child does not crave to be "tucked in" by mother or father, accompanied by a song or a story? Once such times of quiet visiting have been established as routine, they will readily lend themselves to different forms of communication.

The older child no longer asks for parent entertainment but still will be glad to have the parent just to himself for a little while. Here is the opportunity for a dialogue in which the parent can be "on call" without straining. The relaxed atmosphere of the bedtime visit facilitates requests for information and attempts at answers which might not be made in less favorable circumstances. But the ritual of the visit has the further merit of allowing the child to try out his own understandings of his life situation. In the presence of an interested and sympathetic listener he can hear himself say how he feels about himself, about his relationships, and also about his adoption. On one such occasion a twelve-year-old girl confided to her father that the small sister of one of her friends had recently been annoyingly inquisitive. "Why did you not stay with your real mother and father?" she had asked. "I kept quiet," the child told her father, "what could I say?" He agreed that he probably could not have answered either; but letting her know how deeply he felt with her in this predicament, he said: "At times it must be pretty hard being an adopted child." "Yes it is," she answered, "but I'm not sorry."

On this note of cautious optimism we shall rest our case.

CONCLUSION

Our account of the adoptive relationship has been confined to the type in which adopters and adopted had no kinship ties before they came together. The account began with an identification of handicaps that mark various phases of the parent-child relationship. It then pointed to ways in which parents seek to cope with handicap. An assessment of the relative utility of different modes of coping led to a theory of adoptive relations. Our account ended with attempts at specifying how the theory might be put to work. The book was called *Shared Fate* because this title suggests mutual needs and mutual aid. Some things in fate are unalterable; others can be modified by men's active intelligence. Certain strains are given in adoptive relations. How these strains are met and coped with would seem to depend largely on the pioneering spirit of the adoptive parents. In Mannheim's words, ". . . reflectiveness preserves life by helping us to adjust ourselves to situations so complex that in them the naive and unreflective man would be utterly at a loss."

Postscript, 1983

As the preface to this new edition has noted, *Shared Fate* was originally written in the impersonal style then expected of social science monographs. As a result, a number of events that happened in my personal life and the life in my family were camouflaged and made anonymous. Today, two decades later, I am at liberty to speak more personally, and this for two reasons: first of all there is now less pretense of total objectivity in social science writings, for we recognize that the observer of social events is bound to bring his or her own person into the report. It is therefore just as well that the reader gets to know what the reporter's interests and attachments are, for they will necessarily influence the report itself. Secondly I am free to speak more personally in 1983 than I could in 1963 because my children are no longer between ten and twelve years old but between thirty and thirty-two. Even if I had obtained their permission in 1963 for revelations to illustrate the dynamics of adoptive parent-child relationships, such revelations would have been irresponsible due to their ages. Today my children have had opportunities to see my writings and make decisions on what may or may not be revealed. That is how it ought to be, and that is what I have done. In the sequel to *Shared Fate* (*Adoptive Kinship,* 1981, 1984) I have been able to be much more candid than in the present book about the personal experiences that were involved in the journey of discovery to the Shared Fate theory. But I do not want to end this new edition in the impersonal manner in which it was originally written. There is an addition to the theory—really a limitation of it—which I intend to approach in the context of a set of personal events. This limitation of the theory concerns the biological-genetic-constitutional heritage of our children. This heritage we can perhaps come to understand; certainly we must accept it. What we can not do is change it. Even acknowledging differences, empathizing with our children's condition, and opening ourselves to their communications will at best bring them, *with their heritage,* into the community of our family. In this postscript I shall describe how this was brought home to me many years ago.

The cover of this new editon was designed and drawn by my daughter Francie. I had given her the gist of what I wanted, namely the adoptive parents as the ground (Kurt Lewin would have called them the "social ground") on which the adopted children are standing. (Francie's drawing depicts not just four children but fairly close likenesses of herself and her sister and brothers as preteens.) I had spoken of the birth parents and the ancestors of the blood as looking into the lives of the adopted as concerned outsiders. I am grateful to Francie and her artist's imagination for that presentation, so close to the spirit of Shared Fate.

With Francie's permission I want to discuss here some aspects of her early development. These concern in the first place her artistic gifts, and in the second place my resistance to recognizing that they could have been inherent in her.

Francie was almost four months old when Ruth Kirk and I brought her home to Ithaca from Elmira, N.Y. where she had been born and where she had been in a foster home. She was not a particularly beautiful baby, but at the time she seemed to us the most wonderful creature in the world. We would stand over her crib and playpen, watching her every move, playing with and singing to her and enjoying her responses even to the burps after her meals. I am sure I need not explain this kind of infatuation: all people long deprived of children will have similar experiences with the first involvement in parenthood.

Weeks before Francie's arrival in the old house we were renting we had prepared a tiny room for her. The room overlooked a lovely garden full of bluebells and hollyhocks, foxgloves and roses, so that, from any place, looking out of the window, there was a medley of colors, and garden odors, and an aura of welcome. For us it was a very special room already, but thinking of the baby who would spend her nights here we wanted the walls to welcome her as well. We had therefore gone out to find a wallpaper with a simple but colorful recurring pattern. What we found and put on the walls was a jolly Pennsylvania-Dutch design: a red heart, a green leaf, and a blue bird alternating in a diamond space. We had painted a second-hand crib, and on the new mattress there lay, ready and waiting for the occupant-to-be, a small patchwork quilt made some years earlier by Ruth's maternal grandmother for our first child. On that day in late April 1951 the occupant arrived. Shortly thereafter began a series of events that have left their ripple effects on my life.

One evening, perhaps a week after Francie's arrival, Ruth motioned for me to join her at the crib where Francie had just been put to bed. We stood at the head of the crib, Ruth pointing at the baby's hand pulling at the patchwork quilt. Soon the quilt had come over the baby's chin; there was a little hill of cloth before her eyes. The hand seemed to follow the seams of the patches. When we returned to our sitting room Ruth remarked that she thought our baby had a vivid sense of color. I laughed; hadn't my class in psychology and child development indicated that an infant at four months could be expected in the normal course of events to explore the environment? Then the ridges of the quilt's patch seams would be providing the tactile experiences that would satisfy such explorations. Ruth countered with her observations: Francie seemed to put herself to sleep by pulling the coverlet close to her eyes and tracing the colored patterns, *not always identical with the seams.* What mattered to me in all this was whether the recurrent play with the quilt was based principally on the search for tactile or for visual experiences. My textbook learning suggested that the baby's explorations were at that stage tactile. Ruth, less concerned with academic certitudes than with observational evidence, stood her ground. She insisted that I take a look again, and again; I recall that I resisted recognizing what was clearly in front of my nose: our baby was not simply tracing a seam but following colored patterns. After a while the novelty wore off for both of us. Francie and her going-to-sleep habits had become part of our everyday lives.

In the growth process nothing stands still though. It is we who become so used to recurring events that, though once noteworthy, they become ordinary. One day, perhaps three weeks after Francie's arrival, Ruth drew my attention to the fact that the baby was now able to turn over onto her side. I went to her room to watch; what I now saw made the patchwork quilt happenings seem a mild beginning.

The crib had been placed sideways against the wall with the Pennsylvania-Dutch wallpaper design. After some moments Francie stirred, moved over toward the wall, reached her arm (I don't recall which one) through the bars and began to trace the heart. Up her little hand went from the point to the cleavage, and down again, over and over until the arm dropped and the baby was asleep. Ruth tucked Francie's arm under the quilt, turned to me as if to say 'well, what about that?' and we withdrew. I don't know whether it was that same evening that I protested that the wallpaper design probably had some raised edges, perhaps unnoticeable to our calloused fingers but recognizable to the baby's. Actually I must have known better; it was becoming increasingly clear even to me that the baby was tracing the heart *visually* along its red border. What is more, that is how Francie now sent herself off to sleep evening after evening. It was no longer the quilt and its pattern but rather the wall and *its* pattern that served as her security and sleep "blanket".

How acute and accurate Ruth's observations had been became evident a few weeks later. In late May we rented a log cabin in the nearby state park. The crib, the baby, and a few camping utensils more than filled up our little car for the five mile trip to the cabin. By afternoon we were set up, the baby was playing on a blanket on the cabin floor, we were reading or beginning to prepare a meal. To us it quickly felt like home. After our simple supper and the baby's bed-time bottle we sat watching the daylight wane and Francie settling down in her crib. After a while we saw her turn to the left side where her bedroom wall would have been, and where that evening there were just the hewn logs. Francie looked, put out her hand, withdrew it, tried again and stayed awake one hour, two hours, and eventually fell asleep from utter exhaustion.

Ruth remarked that she would go into town and look in our attic for a leftover bit of the wallpaper. What for, I objected; what would it prove but the baby's dependence on her accustomed surroundings? Undeterred, Ruth had brought the remains of a roll of the wallpaper. With Francie playing on the cabin floor, Ruth attached a strip of the paper to the left side of the crib. That night Francie was put to bed at her usual time. As I recall it, she lay placidly on her back for quite some time, eyes open. We were sitting nearby, reading and intermittently watching. After a while the baby turned on her left side and, spotting the wallpaper gave a little cry, ran her fingers along the heart's border, and shortly was asleep.

As I write about these events now I cannot help wondering at my attitude. Why would I not welcome such developments in our baby with excitement and pleasure? Why had I been so rigidly attached to a textbook dogma* instead of observing and noting our baby's actual behavior? I think now that the answer has to be found in my own history and the era in which I received my first university instruction in social science. It was the end of World War II. The racist theories of the Nazi movement and regime, and the murderous consequences of these theories, had left their mark on American social science. Race and heredity went hand-in-hand; so did culture and learning. Accordingly, ethnicity and heredity became minimized in the assessment of human personality and capacity, while culture, environment, and learning became the keys to human functioning.

As Jewish refugees, my parents had found a home in America. Thus for me, the post-war university student, the social science emphasis on environment over heredity proved entirely congenial. In 1951, as a graduate student of sociology, with a tiny adopted daughter in our care, the environmentalist mode of thought about human development satisfied me along several lines. It fitted my academic assumptions, my family history, and now also my self-picture as adoptive father: as long as I emphasized our baby's learning in the present and the future and de-emphasized her genetic and constitutional makeup I could think of myself and our domestic environment as the principal forces that would shape her life. Had I allowed that Francie's early interest in colors and shapes could come from *inside her* I would have had to go against both my social science training (as I understood it then) and against my interest as adoptive father (as I understood *it* then).

Now I must once more return to the wallpaper. By mid-June we were back at our house in Ithaca, making plans for the long railroad trip to California to introduce the baby to our parents. As we could not afford the privacy of a bedroom or even bunks in the sleeping car we anticipated with some trepidation the three days

*Only in recent years has it been found that quite early on in the infant's life visual perception is far more acute than had been believed in the 1950s, so that the infant's experiences of the outer world need not depend solely on tactile sensory explorations.

and nights with the baby in coach accommodations. Reclining seats would give us a minimum of comfort; what must we do to make the journey possible for five months old Francie? There was her car bed; we brought it along in the hope of being able to suspend it from the luggage rack and fit it into the space between two seat backs. It worked, and Francie now had a firm and safe haven. While rigging up this unusual contraption we became the focus of other passengers' interest. The baby, worn out from the long wait between trains in Chicago, was sucking on her bottle when I saw Ruth open a suitcase and take out a length of the wallpaper. I remember feeling annoyed: we didn't need that additional bit of public attention, I thought. But soon Ruth had the shade pulled down on Francie's left side and the wallpaper pinned to it. Once a blanket had been hung around the car bed I decided to ignore the attention we were getting and settled into a book. Not long afterwards Francie had fallen asleep, apparently aided by the familiar wallpaper by her side. The rest of the journey was uneventful, except for the interest that the baby evoked among the other travellers during the day, and which brought us more offers of babysitting than we needed for brief meal visits to the dining car. True, the wallpaper had been noticed, it had raised a few good-natured laughs, but it had also made the tiresome trip by coach bearable, since it had helped Francie to get her naps and her nights' sleep.

Let me now skip over Francie's infancy. In November 1952 we adopted Peter who was just about to turn two. Francie was his junior by about six weeks but, having been the first arrival with so much more social ground under her, she soon became the 'dominant twin'. In the meantime I had received my degree and begun a teaching career in Canada. Among my new acquaintances at Montreal's McGill University was Arthur Lismer, professor of art and director of the Montreal Museum of Fine Arts. He was known as a member of the 'Group of Seven', all painters who earlier in the century had developed an indigenous style of modern Canadian naturalism. Lismer, like his colleagues in the group, was an innovator. He had taken his creative talents beyond the studio into public education. At the museum he had introduced children's art classes, taught by some of his own university students. When we learned of these Saturday morning art classes, they appeared just right for Francie and Peter. It was the Winter of 1956: they were bored with kindergarten and ready for school but would not be admitted until the Fall of 1957. Both were avid 'artists' whose 'work' was hanging everywhere in the house. When we suggested that they join the museum class they were excited, especially because it meant a bus trip to the city and a weekly adventure, by themselves, with their daddy.

So on Saturday mornings in October I was regularly taking Peter and Francie into Montreal for their art class. I would be at my office or the library before it was time to collect the children and take them home. About a month after our weekly routine had become established we heard the first rumblings of displeasure with the class. There had previously been stories of what various children had drawn, for all of them typically produced their crayon and finger paintings on large pieces of butcher paper. Now suddenly there were tears instead of reports. But what it was all about we could not at first discover. By the beginning of December, just before the Christmas holidays, both children announced that they did not want to return. The brief adventure had ended.

Early in 1957, shortly after the new term had begun, I chanced to meet Arthur Lismer at the Faculty Club. He remarked that he was sorry that my children had not cared for the class. I was about to make a quip about strong-headed kids, when Lismer, on his way out called back: "look me up at the museum, I have something to show you." My curiosity aroused, I made an appointment and went to see Professor Lismer at his Museum office a week or so later.

The tall white-haired Lismer motioned me to draw up a chair close to his desk while he was rummaging in one of its drawers. When he found what he had been looking for he put it in front of him and covered it with a blank piece of paper. "First let me tell you what happened," he said. He had gotten the word from one of the young women instructors of the children's class. Apparently some weeks before Christmas the children had been taken up to the lookout on Mount Royal, overlooking the southern part of the city. The teacher had pointed out the dome of the cathedral and the spires of other churches and had announced that as soon as the group returned to the museum they would begin to draw church towers and church windows. Now Arthur Lismer removed the blank sheet of paper covering the item he had located in his desk drawer. "Look what your daughter did with the teacher's suggestion," he said while he pushed a piece of the brown butcher paper in front of me. There it was, unmistakingly a drawing of Francie's. At first I recognized it merely by the psychedelic combination of crayon colors, but as I looked more closely I saw that the intricate pattern was part of what looked like a damaged gothic stained glass window. I say "damaged" because the tip was broken off and hanging from one side. It was like no child's drawing I had ever seen. As I sat there I could not help think of the fact that Francie had been born a couple of days after Christmas and that since her fourth year she had repeatedly asked about her adoption, especially why her birthmother had given her up. Could it be, I asked myself, that the broken window signified in some way my little daughter's awareness of her ruptured family history? I spoke none of these thoughts out loud. As far as I knew Arthur Lismer was not aware of the fact that our children were adopted and I saw no reason for telling him then.

Professor Lismer interrupted my contemplation of Francie's drawing: "There's something uncanny about that gothic window," he said. "It's not just the remarkable conception of the broken tip, but the way she executed it." Now he brought out a piece of tracing paper, followed the outline of Francie's drawing, and filled in with colored pencils the sections closest to the ruptured line. Then he cut along the outline of the tracing paper's window, and also cut the edges where the window was broken. Placing the two pieces of "window" on a white sheet of paper, Arthur Lismer now fitted the broken tip onto the main trunk. I will never forget his triumphal look and my own astonishment. The broken edges fitted almost perfectly together, and the colored pattern continued in the broken tip where it had left off in the main trunk! I tried to take the original from the table, to show it at home, but Lismer whisked it away from me.

"That stays here," he said firmly*. "It will be a reminder to me of what one means by the words 'a born artist'." Then I learned the rest of the story. The children in the art class, seeing this unusual rendition of a church window, had laughed. It was not the first time that Francie's peculiar surrealism had provoked their merriment. Francie had apparently understood the laughter as ridicule. She had stormed out of the studio in a rage. This time it had apparently been the last straw and Peter, faithful brother that he was, had followed. Arthur Lismer's final counsel was against art instruction for a child like Francie. Encouraged to draw and paint she would find her own way in time. It was good advice; in her mid-twenties, having painted for years, she became a student at the Ontario College of Fine Arts.

What does this story of Francie and her apparently inborn artist's perception have to do with this book and this postscript? I have told it here because I was once a "rejection-of-difference" parent who could not allow for his child's inborn world to be admitted into the adoptive family world. By admitting our children's genetic and constitutional heritage we admit also their ancestors. Without doing so we shut off a part of our children's lives, not only against them but against ourselves. The Shared Fate theory and method is thus a key to bringing our children's worlds, liabilities as well as assets, into the world of the adoptive family.

*Many years later, after Arthur Lismer's death, I inquired at the Museum whether Francie's drawing might be located among his papers. I was told that there were many crates of his papers, still unsorted, in the museum's basement. Lack of funds made it impossible to sort or edit them.

APPENDIX A

*

Notes on an Eleven-Item Guttman Scale of the Attitudes of Others As Recalled by Adoptive Parents (Mail Questionnaire Data 1956)

*

Question: **"Here is a list of some reactions which might at times be experienced by adoptive parents and children. For each kind of statement please check the appropriate columns to show whether something like it has been experienced by someone in your family, and if it has happened, how frequently . . ."**

ITEMS (*in scale order*)	*Frequency with which item was reported to have been experienced "frequently" or "occasionally"*
The mother of your child's playmate remarks: "It's hard enough to know how to handle my Johnny when he's giving me trouble. I often wonder how	

you deal with the troublesome behavior of a child who's adopted."	62
You overhear someone saying: "Isn't it wonderful that he can be such a good father to a little boy who isn't his own son."	135
You are being introduced at a party and your host remarks: "They are those unselfish people with the adopted child."	171
A visitor says: "It surely takes a special gift to love someone else's child like your own."	254
A woman says: "How lucky you are that you didn't have to go through all the trouble of pregnancy and birth like *I* had."	478
A neighbor remarks: "How well you care for your child; just like a real mother."	335
A well-wisher says: "He *is* a darling baby, and after all you never know for sure how your own will turn out."	823
A friend asks: "Tell me, do you know anything about this child's background?"	1,227
Someone refers to your adopted child saying, "He (she) is certainly lucky to have you for parents."	1,299
An acquaintance remarks: "Isn't it wonderful of you to have taken this child!"	1,383
A friend says: "This child looks so much like you, he (she) could be your own."	1,373

Scale Notes Responses of "frequently" and "occasionally" were regarded as positive; "just once" and "don't know whether it happened" were regarded as negative. When so treated, the material formed a scale.

Item (e), "Your child is asked by a playmate: 'But who are your *real* parents?' " had more error than nonerror in one response category; hence it was eliminated. Coefficient of Reproducibility = 0.92.

APPENDIX B

*

Indices of Coping Activity (Orientation toward "Acknowledgment-of-Difference")

*

1. *"Relative Deprivation"*

   QUESTION: "Do you feel that other parents have satisfactions that adoptive parents don't have?"

   ANSWER: Yes = "Acknowledgment-of-difference" No = "Rejection-of-difference"

2. *"Relative Deprivation"*

   QUESTION: "Do you feel that you (your wife) have missed an important experience in not bearing own children?"

   ANSWER: Yes = "Acknowledgment-of-difference" No = "Rejection of-difference"

3. *Sameness-Difference (S-D) Score:*

   QUESTION: "In many situations, the feelings of an adoptive parent are just like those of any parent; in other situations, the feelings of adoptive parents may well be different. For each situation listed here, please tell me whether you would expect adoptive parents to have the same feelings as natural parents would have or whether you think their feelings would differ."

SITUATIONS:

a. When a child is expected but hasn't yet arrived;
b. When the relatives meet the child;
c. When someone comments on whether or not the child resembles the parents;
d. When the parent sees his/her preschool child playing with his/her sexual organs;
e. When the child wants to know where babies come from;
f. When discussing children and their problems with a neighbor;
g. When the child has a birthday party;
h. When the child starts school;
i. When the child is sick;
j. When the child gets into trouble with other children or is teased by them;
k. During adolescence, when parents are generally pushed aside in the child's search for independence;
l. When the child contemplates marriage;
m. When the child is grown-up and married and the first grandchild is born.

For each judgment of "different," a score of 1 was given. The number of these "different" judgments were then added together and this sum represented a respondent's S-D score.

4. *Acknowledgment-of-Difference (A-D) Score:*

QUESTIONS	*A score of 1 for each reply suggesting "Acknowledgment"*
"In your opinion do adoptive parents have some satisfactions which other parents do not have?"	"Yes"
"And now, what about other parents? Do you feel that they have satisfactions that adoptive parents don't have?"	"Yes"
"At what times, or in what circumstances are you most keenly aware of the fact that you are an *adoptive* parent?"	Any answer giving times or circumstances
"Have you any special family ceremonies or special days to celebrate, connected with adoption?"	"Yes"

"Now a question about your child's original parents. How often would you say you think about them—frequently, just once in a while, or never?"	"Frequently" or "Once in a while."
"It is apparently not unusual for people at times to feel that they might have been happier with some other child than the one they have. In your opinion, is this feeling more likely to occur in families *without* adopted children, or in families *with* adopted children?"	"Without" or "With"
("From an earlier study of attitudes, we learned that some people in the community seem to look on the adoptive family as being different in some ways from other families. Since some people see it this way . . .")	
"Would you say it is all right for adoptive families to be frankly different by adopting children whose *ages* make it clear that they couldn't have been born to the same mother?"	"Yes"
To the sum obtained from these answers was added the summary score from the S-D test.	S-D Score

The sum obtained from all answers represents a respondent's A-D score.

APPENDIX C

*

Indices of Communication and Gratification

*

INDEX OF COMMUNICATION

1. *Communication of Ideas*

QUESTION: "Now a question about your child's original parents; how often would you say you think about them—frequently, just once in a while, or never?"

(Never to think about the natural parents implies that they cannot be discussed with the child; to think of them occasionally at least means that the basis of communication exists.)

2. *Communication of Feelings* (*Empathy*)

QUESTIONS	*A score of 1 for each reply suggesting empathy*
"It is probably true that people generally have satisfaction in being parents. In your opinion do adoptive parents have some satisfactions which other parents do not have?" (*IF ANSWER IS "YES":*) *What kind of satisfactions for instance do adoptive parents have?*	"Yes" (plus) satisfaction in relationship with child; in giving, filling need of child.

"Have you any special family ceremonies or special days to celebrate, connected with adoption?"	"Yes" or "No" (plus) unsolicited explanation given in terms of child's need.
"Many of those adoptive parents who *tell* their children that they are adopted, find the telling difficult. Why do you suppose it is hard for these adoptive parents to tell their children of their adoption?"	The child's feelings and/ or relationship of adoptive parent to child seen threatened by telling.
"While some (adoptive parents) think it best for adopted children to be told early and repeatedly that they are adopted, (other) adoptive parents do not necessarily agree that this is always best. . . ."	
"In your own case, have you told your child(ren) about adoption?" (IF "YES":) At what age?	At four or younger *or* on arrival if child older when adopted.
"In telling their children of the adoption, some adoptive parents offer reasons why adoption sometimes is necessary. How about you—do you tell your child a reason?"	"Yes"
"Do you think it is generally desirable for an adopted child to learn some of the reasons that people can have for giving their children for adoption?"	"Yes,"—*if child asks or shows need.*
"Have you ever found yourself trying to imagine how your child feels about being adopted?"	"Yes"

The sum obtained from all answers represents a respondent's empathy score.

INDEX OF GRATIFICATION

"Relative Satisfaction"

QUESTION: "In your opinion, do adoptive parents have some satisfactions which other parents do not have?"

APPENDIX D

*

Summary of Mechanisms of Coping with Role Handicap

*

Coping mechanisms with apparently similar objectives have been placed side by side.

"Rejection of Difference"	*"Acknowledgment of Difference"*
Changed Identity and Role	Reaching for New Symbols of Identity and Role
	Desires for New Forms of Sanction
Infancy Adoption	Adoption of Older Children
Simulation of the Biological Family	The Heterogeneous Family
Guarding Adoption Secrets from Outsiders	Announcement-Explanation-Education
	Evangelism-Recruitment
	Group Membership as Role Support

Myth of Origin Defining Child's Status	Celebration of Adoption Anniversary
Removal of Natural Parents' Image	Admission of Natural Parents' Image
Shielding Child from His Origins	Reciprocity in Parent-Child Problems
	Empathy in Parent-Child Problems
	Empathy with Child's Natural Parents
	Empathy with Adopted Child
"Forgetting" the Adoption	Recall of Relative Deprivation
	Recall of Relative Satisfaction
Myth of Origin Defining the Adopters' Status	Emerging Role Models

Bibliography

Barker Foundation, Unpublished Report on Self-Study.

Bedoukian, M., Casault, M., Cherow, M., Linck, P., Schiff, S., Singer, L., and Townshend, R., *Adaptations to Adoptive Parenthood,* Unpublished M.S.W. group thesis, McGill University, 1958.

Boas, F., "The Central Eskimo," *Sixth Annual Report, Bureau of Ethnology,* Government Printing Office, 1888.

Bowlby, J., *Maternal Care and Mental Health,* World Health Organization, 1951.

Bramble, R., Hartman, V., Sewell, E., Friedman, C., and Ouimet, S., *An Exploration Into Some of the Attitudes in the Community Surrounding the Adoptive Family,* Unpublished M.S.W. group thesis, McGill University, 1957.

Brenner, R., *A Follow-Up Study of Adoptive Families,* Child Adoption Research Committee, New York, 1951.

Brooks, L. M., and Brooks, E. C., *Adventuring in Adoption,* Chapel Hill, University of North Carolina Press, 1939.

Brown, F. G., "Services to Adoptive Parents After Legal Adoption," *Child Welfare,* XXXVIII, No. 7 (1959), 16-22.

Cady, E., *We Adopted Three,* New York, William Sloane Associates, 1952, and London, Ernest Benn, Ltd.

Carson, R., *So You Want To Adopt A Baby,* Public Affairs Pamphlet No. 173, 1951.

Child Study Association of America, *What to Tell Your Children About Sex,* copyright under title *Facts of Life for Children,* Maco Magazine Corporation, New York, N.Y. Reprinted by permission of the publisher.

Children's Bureau, *When You Adopt A Child,* Folder No. 13, 1947.

———, *Child Welfare Statistics,* Series No. 66, U.S. Department of Health, Education, and Welfare, 1962.

Clare, J. E., and Kiser, C. V., "Social and Psychological Factors Affecting Fertility—XIV. Preferences for Children of Given Sex in Relation to Fertility," *Milbank Memorial Fund Quarterly,* XXIX, No. 4 (1951), 440-492.

Colby, M. R., *Problems and Procedures in Adoption,* U.S. Children's Bureau Publication No. 262, 1941.

Conklin, E. S., "The Foster-Child Fantasy," *American Journal of Psychology* (January, 1920), Vol. 31, 59-76.

Cynberg, R., Feldman, H., Fillion, J., Fogel, N., Gold, S., Jolley, E. H., Kruger, E., and Workman, G., *Insights Into Adoption,* Unpublished M.S.W. group thesis, McGill University, 1958.

Davies, V., *Tables Showing Significance of Difference Between Percentages and Between Means,* Department of Rural Sociology, Pullman, State College of Washington, 1951.

Davis, K., "Illegitimacy and the Social Structure," *American Journal of Sociology,* XLVI, No. 2 (1939), 215-233.

———, "The Forms of Illegitimacy," *Social Forces,* XVIII, No. 1 (1939), 77-89.

Dinitiz, S., Dynes, R. R., and Clarke, A. C., "Preference for Male and Female Children: Traditional or Affectional?" *Marriage and Family Living,* XVI, No. 2 (1954), 123-130.

Dinkel, R. M., "Attitudes of Children Toward Supporting Aged Parents," *American Sociological Review,* IX (1944), 370-379.

Doss, H., *The Family Nobody Wanted,* Boston, Little, Brown & Co., 1954.

Feldman, H., and J. Meyerowitz, "Development of the Marital Relationship—The First Child Study," supported by N.I.H. grant MH02931. Study in progress.

Firth, R., *We, The Tikopia,* London, George Allen & Unwin, 1936.

Glick, P. G., *American Families,* New York, John Wiley & Sons, 1957.

Goffman, E., *The Presentation of Self in Everyday Life,* New York, Doubleday Anchor Books, 1959.

Goodacre, I., Unpublished Pilot Survey Report from Great Britain.

Gordon, I., "Adoptionen als soziologisches und fürsorgerisches Problem," *Hamburger Wirtschafts- und Sozialwissenschaftliche Schriften,* Rostock, Carl Hinstorffs, 1930.

Guttman, L., "A Basis for Scaling Qualitative Data," *American Sociological Review,* IX, No. 2 (1944), 139-150.

Health, Education, and Welfare Trends, 1962 Edition, U.S. Department of Health, Education, and Welfare.

Jolowicz, A. R., "The Hidden Parent," U.S. Children's Bureau, mimeographed (n.d.).

Kirk, H. D., "A Dilemma of Adoptive Parenthood: Incongruous Role Obligations," *Marriage and Family Living,* XXI, No. 4 (1959), 316-326.

———, *Community Sentiments in Relation to Child Adoption,* Unpublished Ph.D. thesis, Cornell University, 1953.

———, "Guarding the Ramparts—Reader Reactions to a Magazine Article Questioning a Social Work Prescription," *The Social Worker* (June-July 1962), 31-43.

———, "Nonfecund People as Parents," *Fertility and Sterility,* XIV, No. 3 (1963), 310-319.

———, *Parent-Child Relations in Adoption,* McGill University School of Social Work, 1961, mimeographed.

Kirkpatrick, C., *The Family as Process and Institution,* New York, The Ronald Press, 1955.

Klein, J., *The Study of Groups,* London, Routledge and Kegan Paul, Ltd., 1956. Reprinted by permission of the publisher.

Kornbluth, R., A. Laws, J. MacFarlane, R. Manson, E. G. Nemeth, *Some Aspects of What Is Important to Adoptive Parents,* unpublished M.S.W. group thesis, McGill University, 1957.

Kornitzer, M., *Child Adoption in the Modern World,* London, Putnam & Co. Ltd., 1952.

Leahy, A., "Some Characteristics of Adoptive Parents," *American Journal of Sociology* (1933), Vol. 38, 548-563.

Lemon, E. M., "Rear View Mirror; An Experience with Completed Adoptions," *The Social Worker* (June-July 1959), Vol. 27, 41-51.

Lewin, K., "Bringing Up the Child," *The Menorah Journal,* XXVIII, No. 1 (1940), 29-45; reprinted under the title "Bringing Up the Jewish Child," in K. Lewin, *Resolving Social Conflicts,* New York, Harper & Row Publishers, Inc., 1948. Reprinted by permission of the publisher.

Louisiana Department of Public Welfare, *How To Adopt A Child in Louisiana,* 1950.

Lowie, R., "Adoption—Primitive," *Encyclopedia of the Social Sciences,* Vol. I, 459-460, The Macmillan Company, 1930.

Malinowski, B., "Myths in Primitive Psychology," in *Magic, Science and Religion,* New York, Doubleday Anchor Books, 1954.

MacLeod, M. A., *All About You—An Adopted Child's Memory Book,* Norwalk, Conn., C. R. Gibson & Co., 1959.

Mannheim, K., *Man and Society in an Age of Reconstruction,* New York, Harcourt, Brace & World, Inc., 1950. Reprinted by permission of the publisher.

Myrdal, G., *An American Dilemma,* New York, Harper & Row Publishers, Inc., 1944.

Neely, W. C., "Family Attitudes of Denominational College and University Students, 1929-1936," *American Sociological Review,* V (1940), 512-522.

New Jersey State Board of Child Welfare, *Adoptions Take Time,* 1947.

Oklahoma State Department of Social Welfare, Child Welfare Division, *So You Want To Adopt a Child* (n.d.).

Patai, R., *Sex and Family in the Bible and the Middle East,* New York, Doubleday Dolphin Books, 1959.

Paton, J. M., *The Adopted Break Silence,* Life History Study Center, Acton, California, 1954.

———, *Three Trips Home,* Life History Study Center, Acton, California, 1960.

Riesman, D., "A Philosophy for 'Minority' Living," in D. Riesman, *Individualism Reconsidered,* New York, The Free Press of Glencoe, 1954.

Rockwood, L. R., and Ford, M. E. N., *Youth, Marriage and Parenthood,* New York, John Wiley & Sons, Inc., 1945. Reprinted by permission of the publisher.

Sandgrund, G., "Group Counseling With Adoptive Families After Legal Adoption," *Child Welfare,* XLI, No. 6 (1962), 248-252.

Sarbin, T. R., "Role Theory," In G. Lindsey (ed.), *Handbook of Social Psychology,* Reading, Mass., Addison-Wesley Publishing Co., Inc., 1954.

Schapiro, M., *A Study of Adoption Practice,* Vol. I, Child Welfare League of America, Inc., 1956.

Seeman, M., "On the Meaning of Alienation," *American Sociological Review,* XXIV (1959), 783-791.

Theis, S. V. S., *How Foster Children Turn Out,* State Charities Aid Association, New York, 1924.

Thunen, M., "Ending Contact with Adoptive Parents; The Group Meeting," *Child Welfare,* XXXVII, No. 2 (1958), 8-14.

Wasson, V. P. *The Chosen Baby, Philadelphia,* Lippincott, 1950.

Weckler, J. E., "Adoption on Mokil," *American Anthropologist,* LV, No. 4 (1953), 555-568.

Index

*

A Note on the Author

H. DAVID KIRK was born in 1918 into a Jewish family in the Rhineland, West Germany. The family name was Kirchheimer, anglicized when the parents took the three sons to the United States in 1938. In 1934 David had left Germany to finish high school in England. Later, in America, he earned a B.S. degree at the City College of New York. During 1948 to 1953 he was a graduate student at Cornell University, where he was also an instructor and held a research fellowship from the United States Public Health Service. This enabled him to undertake the study of community values concerning illegitimacy, infertility, and adoption, and it led to his Ph.D. dissertation. Although adoption has been his longest-term interest, this interest arose out of the larger issues of human dislocation, belongingness, loyalty, and community, issues of which his boyhood experiences made him aware.

In 1954 he joined the faculty of McGill University's School of Social Work, and a year later he was able to initiate the cross-national survey of adoptive families. From the various studies of that decade there resulted Kirk's first book, *Shared Fate*. A second book, *Adoptive Kinship*, appeared in 1981, supplementing the ideas developed in the earlier one by an analysis of adoption laws and policies. Professor Kirk is currently a member of the Department of Sociology at the University of Waterloo and the Faculty of Law, University of Victoria. He has lectured on adoption in Canada, the United States, Great Britain, Denmark, Germany, Italy, and Israel. He is the adoptive father of four, now in their thirties.